A Teacher Quality Primer
For Michigan School Officials,
State Policymakers, Media and Residents

Mackinac Center for Public Policy

Marc J. Holley

A Teacher Quality Primer
for Michigan School Officials, State Policymakers, Media and Residents
2008 - 1ST EDITION

Marc J. Holley

©2008 by the Mackinac Center for Public Policy
Midland, Michigan

Guarantee of Quality Scholarship

The Mackinac Center for Public Policy is committed to delivering the highest quality and most reliable research on Michigan issues. The Center guarantees that all original factual data are true and correct and that information attributed to other sources is accurately represented.

The Center encourages rigorous critique of its research. If the accuracy of any material fact or reference to an independent source is questioned and brought to the Center's attention with supporting evidence, the Center will respond in writing. If an error exists, it will be noted in an errata sheet that will accompany all subsequent distribution of the publication, which constitutes the complete and final remedy under this guarantee.

Permission to reprint in whole or in part is hereby granted, provided that the Mackinac Center for Public Policy is properly cited.

ISBN-13: 978-1-890624-76-7
ISBN-10: 1-890624-76-4
S2008-05

About the Mackinac Center

The Mackinac Center for Public Policy is a nonpartisan research and educational institute devoted to improving the quality of life for all Michigan residents by promoting sound solutions to state and local policy questions. The Mackinac Center assists policymakers, scholars, business people, the media and the public by providing objective analysis of Michigan issues. The goal of all Center reports, commentaries and educational programs is to equip Michigan residents and other decision-makers to better evaluate policy options. The Mackinac Center for Public Policy is broadening the debate on issues that have for many years been dominated by the belief that government intervention should be the standard solution. Center publications and programs, in contrast, offer an integrated and comprehensive approach that considers:

All Institutions. The Center examines the important role of voluntary associations, communities, businesses and families, as well as government.

All People. Mackinac Center research recognizes the diversity of Michigan residents and treats them as individuals with unique backgrounds, circumstances and goals.

All Disciplines. Center research incorporates the best understanding of economics, science, law, psychology, history and morality, moving beyond mechanical cost-benefit analysis.

All Times. Center research evaluates long-term consequences, not simply short-term impact.

Committed to its independence, the Mackinac Center for Public Policy neither seeks nor accepts any government funding. The Center enjoys the support of foundations, individuals and businesses that share a concern for Michigan's future and recognize the important role of sound ideas. The Center is a nonprofit, tax-exempt organization under Section 501(c)(3) of the Internal Revenue Code. For more information on programs and publications of the Mackinac Center for Public Policy, please contact us.

140 West Main Street, P.O. Box 568, Midland, Mich. 48640; 989-631-0900
Fax 989-631-0964; www.mackinac.org • mcpp@mackinac.org

Contents

Acknowledgements

I would like to thank Ryan Olson for his guidance, support and insight. Several peer reviewers generously gave us the benefit of their expertise and meticulously examined a draft of this publication: my thanks to Sandra Stotsky, Dan Goldhaber, Patrick Wolf and Barbara Ruga. This primer reflects the insights and assistance of others as well, including an important legal analysis of the constitutionality of merit pay in Michigan by Mackinac Center Senior Legal Analyst Patrick Wright.

I would also like to thank Gary Ritter, Jay Greene, Bob Costrell, Matthew Carr and, of course, Taylor Holley. The final version of this document reflects many of their fine suggestions and is the better for it, but I remain solely responsible for any errors that remain. I am also grateful to the Mackinac Center for Public Policy's Michael Jahr, Hannah Mead and Daniel Montgomery for their many fine efforts on this project.

Finally, I want to thank the Mackinac Center for Public Policy for its support of, and interest in, this project.

Preface

The education research community now recognizes what many parents have long believed — namely, that of all the factors schools can control, teachers matter most.[i] Policymakers, in turn, are starting to pay attention. The No Child Left Behind Act has attempted to make teacher quality a national priority by requiring all states to certify that students are being taught by "highly qualified" teachers.

However, the characteristics that are used to designate a teacher as highly qualified may not be the ones that actually affect student achievement. While it is true that Michigan students learn a variety of skills in their time at school, perhaps the most important charge of public schools, beyond providing a safe and healthy environment, is to ensure that students are learning their three R's. Unfortunately, the achievement levels of Michigan public school students raise doubts about the quality of public education in the state. This volume has been written to assist policymakers at the state and local levels who want to initiate and support teacher quality reforms to improve K-12 public education in the state.

Many of Michigan's teachers are truly outstanding, and recommending that policymakers concentrate on enhancing the quality of the teaching work force is not an indictment of Michigan's teachers. In fact, it is because teachers are critical to the success of Michigan's students that they are the focus of this work. Perhaps the best way for the state to improve education for its 1.7 million students is to institute greater competition in the form of universal school choice.[ii] However, until the state amends its constitution to permit this reform, Michigan policymakers should focus on upgrading the input most likely to raise the return on their high level of investment in the short term: teachers.

i Dan Goldhaber recently summarized teachers' impact in this way: "Education research convincingly shows that teacher quality is the most important schooling factor influencing student achievement." See Dan D. Goldhaber, "Teacher Pay Reforms" (Center for American Progress: The Political Implications of Recent Research, December 2006), 4, http://www.americanprogress.org/issues/2006/12/pdf/teacher_pay_report.pdf (accessed June 26, 2008).

ii For information about school choice, see Matthew J. Brouillette, "School Choice in Michigan: A Primer for Freedom in Education" (Mackinac Center for Public Policy, 1999), 1-66, http://www.mackinac.org/archives/1999/s1999-06.pdf (accessed May 7, 2008). See also Lawrence W. Reed, "A New Direction for Education Reform" (Mackinac Center for Public Policy, 2001), http://www.mackinac.org/3541 (accessed May 8, 2008).

Moreover, even when high-quality school choice is more readily available in the state, the teacher quality reforms suggested in this work can be undertaken as complementary reforms. [iii] School choice initiatives and reforming teacher incentives are not mutually exclusive.

In the pages that follow, I begin by describing shortcomings in public education in the state. Next, I briefly describe the research consensus that good teachers matter and explore whether certification, experience, graduate degrees, academic ability and high licensure exam scores make teachers more effective in the classroom. Before using these findings to recommend particular teacher quality reforms, I discuss whether class-size reductions and across-the-board pay raises, two other popular reforms, might be more efficient ways to improve student achievement. Ultimately, the teacher quality reforms described here should help local and state policymakers encourage good teaching and raise student achievement. The book draws on extensive research literature and comprehensive reports to remain current with the latest findings.

The first step in reforming teacher quality is to redefine what being a highly qualified teacher truly means. The words "highly qualified" should no longer refer to a teacher with extensive pedagogical training or years of experience; they should refer to a teacher whose work improves student learning. This redefinition informs our recommendations, which include the following:

- Change the teacher compensation structure by instituting "performance pay" for teachers and rewarding them for gains in student achievement as measured on standardized tests. This merit-based pay structure will motivate existing teachers and attract high-quality undergraduates and career-changers.

- Adopt differential pay, which provides financial rewards to teachers in high-demand fields, such as math and science.

- Lower barriers to entry for career-changers through more reasonable alternative certification programs than Michigan has now.

---

iii   For a discussion of how other education reforms are compatible with greater school choice, see Jay P. Greene's commentary in Jay P. Greene et al., "Is School Choice Enough?" (City Journal, 2008), http://www.city-journal.org/2008/forum0124.html (accessed May 8, 2008).

- Evaluate teachers annually based on principal observations and student achievement gains; loosen restrictions on terminating ineffective teachers; and de-emphasize professional development as it is currently conceived.

Note that these are feasible reforms. Although they may require renegotiating union contracts or changing state certification laws, they do not require constitutional amendments or statewide initiatives. They can be instituted at the first opportunity.

To that end, this book emphasizes reforms immediately available to local school boards or possible through relatively modest changes to state law. Most of these reforms therefore dwell on encouraging quality instruction — and discouraging poor instruction — once teachers have entered the school system. I spend less time on teacher preparation reforms and other restructuring that might improve the quality of candidates entering the teaching work force. Such areas of reform, while also important, would extend well beyond the public school system and require a more extensive discussion than can be provided here.

Yet an important message remains: Teachers are key to student learning. Education policymakers can no longer afford to ignore the reality that teachers respond to incentives and that policies that protect low-performing teachers at the expense of student achievement — and other teachers — need to be replaced.[iv] Michigan's children deserve no less.

---

iv This report does not address the specific strategies and research related to improving teacher quality for specialized instructors, such as reading or special education teachers.

Part I: Michigan Education's Return on Investment

When evaluating whether Michigan's public education system is producing acceptable outcomes, it is important to look at both levels of achievement and levels of spending. If Michigan were spending more than other states but achieving at a higher rate, it might be reasonable to argue that the education system is relatively efficient. One could claim that the state spends more and gets more. Another way to evaluate spending and achievement is to look at trends over time. If the state started at lower levels of student achievement and education spending than other states, but student achievement grew at a faster rate, one could reasonably conclude that the education system was receiving a reasonable return on its investment.

Unfortunately, spending has increased, but student achievement has either remained level or lost ground in national comparisons. Such comparisons are important because single or absolute measures of a state's performance can be misleading. If we were to see that Michigan improved five points on a math exam, for example, we might think there was cause for celebration. However, if the national average gain were nine points, we would rethink that assessment. Alternatively, if Michigan were to lose two points on the reading assessment, we might think that there was cause for concern. However, if the national average dropped eight points, Michigan might not be doing poorly after all.

Additionally, rather than looking exclusively at proficiency levels on a state's own exams, comparisons of student achievement across states should also be made using the National Assessment of Educational Progress exams. Although the federal No Child Left Behind Act mandates that every state test students annually in grades three through eight in math and language arts, states are not required to use any specific test.[v] As a result, states can adopt NCLB exams that are more challenging or less challenging based on their own individual state policies. Moreover, states can set proficiency cut-points at varying levels. These variations make comparisons across states based on state exams particularly difficult.

By contrast, the NAEP exams are nationally administered and uniform for all states. The National Center for Education Statistics in

---

v Strictly speaking, the mandates of the No Child Left Behind Act apply only to those states that accept the federal money tied to the act. Michigan currently accepts this money.

Washington, D.C., draws a representative sample of students in each state and tests them in grades four and eight in math and reading. NCES also periodically administers science and writing tests as a part of the NAEP battery.[1]

NCES processes NAEP test score data and reports student achievement levels on a standardized scale. Graphic 1 below shows a comparison between Michigan students and students nationwide on the fourth-grade NAEP math exam.[2] The figure shows that Michigan students were achieving above the national average in 1996. In subsequent years, average scores improved nationwide, including in Michigan. Unfortunately, Michigan students' scores fell relative to the rest of the nation during the last few years and dropped below the national average in 2007.

Graphic 1: Michigan's Lost Lead in Student Achievement on Grade Four Math National Assessment of Educational Progress Tests

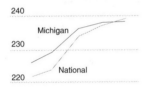

240

Michigan

230

National

220

1996 2000 2003 2005 2007

Source: National Center for Education Statistics

Graphic 2 shows the situation in eighth grade. At this grade level, the performance of Michigan students has remained relatively stable over time. In comparison, however, students nationwide, who performed at a lower level in 1996, have surpassed Michigan students.[vi, 3]

---

vi Average fourth-grade math scores of about 240 and average eighth-grade reading scores of about 280 reflect only that the scales for fourth- and eighth-grade student tests are different, not that eighth-grade students are performing better than fourth-grade students compared to national standards.

Graphic 2: Michigan's Lost Lead in Student Achievement on Grade Eight Math National Assessment of Educational Progress Tests

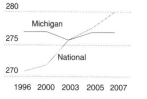

Source: *National Center for Education Statistics*

This story is only marginally better for Michigan students in reading. Graphics 3 and 4 show that Michigan students, once slightly above the national average in fourth- and eighth-grade, are now at or below the national average.[vii]

---

vii The observed differences between Michigan's performance and the national average in Graphics 1-4 are statistically significant at the 95 percent confidence level in some cases. The comparisons in Graphic 1 (grade four math) and Graphic 2 (grade eight math) each contain one statistically significant difference at the 95 percent confidence level between Michigan's performance (higher) and the national performance (lower) before 2007. In both cases, that advantage has been lost. In fact, in Graphic 2 (grade eight math), a lead that was once statistically significant for Michigan students is now a statistically significant disadvantage. In Graphic 3 (grade four reading), the difference between Michigan and the national average approaches statistical significance at the 95 percent confidence level and represents statistical significance at the 90 percent confidence level. The performance of Michigan students in grade four reading is now statistically indistinguishable from the national average. In Graphic 4 (grade eight reading), the difference between Michigan students and the national average has never been statistically significantly at the 95 percent confidence level, but the trend in this subject is consistent with the trend in the other subjects regarding comparisons to the national average. In all, it is safe to say that Michigan students do not compare as favorably to the national average as they once did. These graphics should also be interpreted with reference to the findings in Graphics 5 and 6.

Graphic 3: Michigan's Lost Lead in Student Achievement on Grade Four Reading National Assessment of Educational Progress Tests

Source: *National Center for Education Statistics*

Graphic 4: Michigan's Lost Lead in Student Achievement on Grade Eight Reading National Assessment of Educational Progress Tests

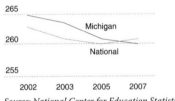

Source: *National Center for Education Statistics*

Some might argue that Michigan students' performance, which is at or only slightly below the national average in math and reading, is acceptable.[viii] Looking at achievement relative to expenditures, however, shifts the perspective.[ix] State education expenditures have increased

---

viii Michigan students have also taken National Assessment of Educational Progress exams in both science and writing. While the science scores are somewhat more encouraging, the number of Michigan students achieving "proficient" and "advanced" scores is not very high. In the NAEP writing exams, Michigan's scores are below average.

ix In Helen F. Ladd, *Holding Schools Accountable: Performance-Based Reform in Education* (Brookings Institution Press, 1996), Ladd argued that looking at increases in spending relative to changes in NAEP scores may overstate the relationship between inputs and outcomes. Specifically, she was relating the trends in national NAEP achievement to changes in education spending between 1971 and 1992. Ladd suggested that it is necessary to deflate spending increases by a factor greater than standard deflators because education inputs have suffered from above-average inflation. In asserting that average students have not had the benefit of greater resources, she also claimed that education spending has also increased due in large part to the growth of special education expenditures. On Page 3, Ladd stated, "[E]ducating children has dramatically over the last two decades. In school year 2004-2005, Michigan spent more than $19.3 billion[4] on primary and secondary public education. Using constant 2005 dollars, that amount reflected an increase of more than 50 percent since school year 1988-1989. Graphic 5 shows the long-term increase in the state's real spending on public education in the years before and during the administration of the NAEP exams charted in Graphics 1 through 4 above.[x, 5]

Graphic 5: Total Real Public Education Spending in Michigan
2005 dollars

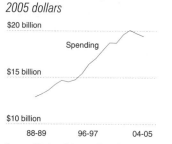

Source: *National Center for Education Statistics and U.S. Bureau of Labor Statistics*

Finally, it is instructive to see how the state ranks in various spending measures and how Michigan students rank in achievement levels.

become more challenging over time because of the increasing proportions of children who are raised in poverty or single-parent households, or both. Hence, some of the increase in resources simply reflects the fact that schools are being asked to do more today than in the past."

Despite Ladd's objections to this manner of discussing the relationship between increased spending and flat test scores, it is undeniable that over the past 15 years student performance in Michigan has not gained ground in national comparisons and that Michigan's spending has been high and rising over the same period. This raises legitimate questions about spending productivity. Ultimately, Ladd did admit that "most people agree that schools need to become more productive in the future" (Ladd, *Holding Schools Accountable: Performance-Based Reform in Education,* 3). This conclusion is exactly the focus of this primer. If a larger proportion of students is becoming more difficult to educate, it is all the more reason to find ways to make education investments work smarter to achieve results.

x In real terms, there were slight annual declines in total spending on primary and secondary public education at various points during the interval shown in Graphic 5. In nominal terms, total spending on public education increased every school year during this period.

Stating that Michigan student performance falls at or near national averages does not reveal where state achievement ranks in comparison to other states. Additionally, the spending figures above do not show Michigan's expenditures relative to other states.

Although Michigan students' 2007 NAEP test scores are close to national averages, they actually rank Michigan students 32nd in eighth-grade reading, 36th in eighth-grade math, 30th in fourth-grade reading and 32nd in fourth-grade math.[6] These results are striking considering that in 2007, Michigan had the eighth-highest average elementary school teacher salaries.[xi, 7] In addition, in 2006 Michigan had the ninth-highest total current spending on schools per $1,000 of personal income, where current spending essentially represents operating expenditures.[xii, 8] Taxpayers are paying disproportionately high amounts for relatively low levels of student achievement (see Graphic 6). Michigan's total current expenditures per pupil has also been relatively high, ranking 16th in the 2004-2005 school year.[9]

---

xi This teacher salary ranking and the salary rankings in Graphic 6 are based on U.S. Bureau of Labor Statistics salary figures for each state. The figures are not adjusted for cost-of-living differences among states for three reasons.

First, a cost-of-living adjustment ratio is best applied regionally and not for a state as a whole. Second, adjusting state average salaries for the cost of living would require computing a weighted average based on the percentage of teachers in each region of each state and the corresponding adjusted average salaries for those regions — a demanding calculation involving multiple assumptions that could represent a research paper in itself. Third, a complete state-by-state comparison regarding teacher compensation would need to account for differences in employee benefits, for which complete data are not readily available. It is likely that such adjustments would not lower the relative ranking of Michigan teachers in national comparisons.

xii The National Center for Education Statistics defines current spending as follows: "This is the sum of expenditures for Instruction, Support Services, Non-instructional Services (excluding Community Services), and Direct Program Support (excluding Support for Private school Students), and excludes Property expenditures."

Graphic 6: The Disparity Between Michigan's Rankings in Spending and Student Achievement

Achievement Rank Among States	Spending Rank Among States
Grade 4 Math — 32nd (2007)	Average Elementary School Teacher Salaries — 8th (2007)
Grade 4 Reading — 30th (2007)	Average Secondary School Teacher Salaries — 11th (2007)
Grade 8 Math — 36th (2007)	Total Current Spending/$1000 Income — 9th (2005-2006)
Grade 8 Reading — 32nd (2007)	Total Current Expenditures Per Pupil — 16th (2004-2005)

Sources: Mackinac Center calculations using National Assessment of Education Progress data; U.S. Bureau of Labor Statistics; and the National Center for Education Statistics. Elementary school teachers exclude special education teachers, and secondary school teachers exclude both special and vocational education teachers.

Part II: Teachers Matter

Researchers of varying views have come to agree that, of factors that schools can control, teachers make the largest difference in a student's education. Teacher quality scholar Dan Goldhaber has succinctly asserted, "It appears that the most important thing a school can do is to provide its students with good teachers."[10] Stanford University's Eric Hanushek and colleagues have conducted several rigorous studies to measure the impacts that teachers have on students and have repeatedly found that teachers matter. Asserting that teachers have profound effects on student achievement, Hanushek and Steven Rivkin wrote, "[A] good teacher will get a gain of 1.5 grade level equivalents while a bad teacher will get 0.5 year for a single academic year."[11] These researchers have also found that effects of teachers last over time; they estimate that "having five years of good teachers in a row (1.0 standard deviation above average, or at the 85th percentile) could overcome the average seventh-grade mathematics achievement gap between lower-income kids (those on the free or reduced-price lunch program) and those from higher-income families."[12]

Although she differs from Hanushek in her views over which characteristics of teachers make them more effective, Stanford's Linda Darling-Hammond agrees that high-quality teachers are important for student success.[13] In turn, political scientist Terry Moe of the Hoover Institute, a scholar who does not regularly concur with Darling-Hammond, also asserts that teachers are essential. In an article suggesting that collective bargaining interferes with providing students with good teachers, Moe writes, "When contract rules make it difficult or impossible to weed out mediocre teachers, for example, they directly undermine the single most important determinant of student learning: teacher quality."[14]

Part III: Assessing Which Teacher Characteristics Are Important

Identifying the characteristics that make teachers effective is the first step in designing policy solutions to improve teacher quality. It is also important to understand which characteristics do not impact teacher effectiveness. With a knowledge of which types of teachers produce student achievement gains, policymakers can design policies to recruit and retain such teachers for Michigan classrooms. Although education researchers agree that teachers matter, they often lament that the specific characteristics that make certain teachers more effective than others are statistically unobservable, given existing data.[15] Despite these limitations on teacher quality research,[xiii] some trends concerning meaningful teacher characteristics have begun to emerge.

A Teacher's Own Academic Ability

As Dale Ballou of Vanderbilt University and Michael Podgursky of the University of Missouri have noted, the weight of the available education research heavily supports the contention that academically able teachers tend to have higher-performing students.[16] Citing ample research evidence, Richard Murnane and Jennifer Steele of the Harvard University Graduate School of Education write, "One teacher characteristic that is somewhat helpful in predicting student outcomes is academic ability, as measured by verbal aptitude scores, ACT scores, or undergraduate college selectivity."[17]

Analyzing student and district data in Alabama, Ronald Ferguson and Helen Ladd measured the contribution that various education inputs make to student achievement. They found that smarter teachers — that is, those who had higher scores on the ACT when they applied to college — were more successful at increasing their students' reading and math scores, with the impact stronger in reading than in math. They wrote, "The 0.10 coefficient for reading implies that a difference of one standard deviation in the distribution of teacher test scores would

---

xiii Other limitations exist as well. In particular, individual studies on teacher quality are often based on data for only a few grade levels. Hence, scholars cannot necessarily assume their findings will be consistent for all grades. Nevertheless, most of the studies included in this primer involve high-quality research by leading scholars in the field. They have designed their studies to be as broadly applicable as possible, thereby increasing the likelihood the results can be generalized across grade levels. As a result, a consensus has developed among scholars about the broad parameters of teaching quality, despite their awareness of the desirability of additional research.

generate a difference of 0.10 standard deviations in the distribution of student test scores."[xiv]

The teaching profession, however, draws disproportionately from the lower end of the distribution of academic ability.[xv] Robin Henke, Xianglei Chen and Sonya Geis of the federal government's National Center for Education Statistics, for instance, analyzed data from the Baccalaureate and Beyond Longitudinal Data Survey.[18] This data set includes information on the characteristics of individuals who had prepared to teach and who had entered the teaching profession in 1993 and on those same individuals' teaching career decisions in 1997. Henke and colleagues showed that college graduates who became teachers were more likely than other college graduates to have scored in the bottom quartile on their college entrance exams.

Writing for the Education Policy Center at Michigan State University, Stanford University education researcher Susanna Loeb and Michelle Reininger, now of Northwestern University, confirmed this finding by studying teachers who graduated from the State University of New York.[19] Loeb and Reininger state that these data "show that elementary and secondary school teachers are more likely to have scored at the lower end of the distribution of SAT scores than non-teachers." As in the study of Henke and colleagues, Loeb and Reininger qualified their findings by showing that teachers of high school math and science are likely to have

---

xiv Ronald Ferguson and Helen F. Ladd, "How and Why Money Matters: An Analysis of Alabama Schools," in *Holding Schools Accountable*, ed. Helen F. Ladd (Brookings Institution, 1996), p. 277. They continue: "Alternatively, the effect of teacher test scores can be compared with the estimated effects of the socioeconomic characteristics of the community. For example, the estimated coefficients imply that it would take an increase of 25 percentage points in the percentage of college-educated adults (which is equivalent to slightly less than a two-standard deviation change) to achieve the same gain in reading test scores that could be obtained by substituting teachers with test scores one standard deviation higher than those of the school's current teachers" (p. 278).

xv Goldhaber, "The Mystery of Good Teaching: Surveying the Evidence on Student Achievement and Teachers' Characteristics." In another paper, Goldhaber observes: "Not surprisingly, the non-teacher labor market again rewards ability at a much higher rate than the teacher labor market, with the teacher labor market actually giving a slight premium to those with the lowest SAT scores in 2004." See Dan D. Goldhaber, "Teacher Pay Reforms" (Center for American Progress, 2006), 8, http://www.americanprogress.org/issues/2006/12/pdf/teacher_pay_report.pdf (accessed May 22, 2008).

scored well on their college entrance exams compared to teachers of other subjects and even to nonteachers. To support their own research, Loeb and Reininger also cited Eric Hanushek and Richard Pace[20] and Emeliana Vegas and colleagues,[21] who had similar findings.[xvi]

The teaching profession also tends to lose those with greater academic ability. Loeb and Reininger pointed out, "[T]eachers with higher test scores are more likely to transfer or quit teaching, leaving behind their lower scoring colleagues."[22] This point is reinforced by Henke and colleagues, who found that 32.1 percent of teachers who had scored in the top quartile on their college entrance exams quit teaching, compared to 16.1 percent of teachers who had scored in the bottom quartile.[23]

One trend affecting the teaching work force is that fewer of the most academically able women are entering the field than in prior generations. Using five longitudinal data sets spanning 35 years, Sean Corcoran, William Evans and Robert Schwab found, "Whereas close to 20 percent of females in the top decile in 1964 chose teaching as a profession (teaching was the most frequently reported occupation among this group in 1964), only 3.7 percent of top decile females were teaching in 1992."[24] These researchers also found a decline in the average teacher's performance on standardized math and verbal tests relative to other female high school graduates. They attributed these declines in teacher quality to enhanced job opportunities for women in other competitive fields. They found, "Top scoring women in our 1992 cohort were much more likely to be working as computer specialists (5.9 percent), accountants (6.0 percent), or managers (15.1 percent). Top decile females were almost as likely to be lawyers (3.2 percent) as teachers."[25]

Analyzing this trend, Caroline Hoxby, now of Stanford University, and Andrew Leigh of The Australian National University found a

---

xvi "... Dan Goldhaber and Albert Liu show that in a sample of recent college graduates, those who report considering a career as a teacher have SAT scores that are, on average, about 40 points lower than those who do not, and college graduates who become teachers have SAT scores that are more than 50 points lower than those who enter a different occupation. ... The differential in aptitude (measured, for instance, by SAT scores) between teachers and non-teachers is certainly a concern given empirical evidence that higher-aptitude teachers tend to be more effective in the classroom" (Goldhaber, "Teacher Pay Reforms," 9-10).

different explanation. Hoxby and Leigh discovered that two factors related to teacher pay have contributed to the loss of more academically able women from the teaching work force. First, from 1963 to 2000, they showed that the wages for women gradually approached those for men across the range of nonteaching professions. Then they demonstrated that wages for teachers with higher academic aptitude fell relative to the average wage for all teachers and that wages for teachers with lower academic aptitude rose relative to the average for all teachers. Their conclusion is informative: "[W]e cannot expect high-performing college graduates to continue to enter teaching if that is the one profession in which pay is decoupled from performance."[26]

Since academically able teachers tend to be successful in promoting student achievement, it is important to find ways to reverse this trend and encourage them to enter and remain in the teaching profession.

Teaching Experience

The education research community has also considered whether teacher experience makes a difference in student achievement. This is an important issue, since existing teacher compensation policies usually reward teachers for staying on the job longer.

By state law, each district in Michigan negotiates its own salary schedule. Most districts have a "single salary schedule," meaning that one schedule determines the wages for all teachers in the district. This compensation policy has been in effect since the early 20th century, and it rewards teachers according to their level of degree and years of experience on the job.[27] In other words, under the single salary schedule, there is no differentiation in pay based on subject area, grade level, the difficult teaching conditions in a particular school within a district, or other teaching conditions. The single salary schedule was initially adopted to remove the possibility for unfair discrimination in teacher pay due to teacher characteristics unrelated to their effectiveness.[28]

As an example, consider an outline of the single salary schedule tentatively agreed to for the 2008-2009 school year by the Ann Arbor Public Schools and the local teachers union (see Graphic 7). Along the rows of the table, teachers are compensated based on their years of experience. In this salary schedule, a new teacher with zero years of experience would be placed at step 1. Along the columns, teachers are compensated according to their academic degrees. Thus, a new teacher with zero years of experience would earn $39,540 for having a bachelor of arts degree, but would earn $44,539 for having a master of arts degree.

Graphic 7: Sample Single Salary Schedule
(Tentative Schedule for Ann Arbor Schools)

SALARY SCHEDULE 2008-2009, 1.75 percent increase over 2007-2008

Degree/ step	BA	BA+30	MA	MA+30 BA+60W/ MA 2 MA	ED. SPEC.	BA+90/ MA	PH.D.
1	$39,540	$43,053	$44,539	$45,934	$47,154	$48,476	$49,919
2	$42,199	$46,019	$47,871	$49,277	$50,513	$51,951	$53,432
3	$44,815	$48,566	$51,235	$52,667	$53,978	$55,453	$57,045
4	$47,393	$51,787	$54,678	$56,164	$57,554	$59,045	$60,738
5	$50,147	$55,448	$58,196	$59,799	$61,210	$62,765	$64,457
6	$52,901	$58,340	$61,873	$63,476	$64,930	$66,511	$68,310
7	$55,697	$62,080	$65,556	$67,285	$68,734	$70,352	$72,199
8	$58,615	$65,428	$69,275	$71,249	$72,809	$74,624	$76,704
9	$61,566	$68,745	$73,053	$75,213	$76,815	$78,948	$81,124
10	$65,662	$73,451	$78,333	$80,025	$81,760	$83,777	$86,053
L1	$66,318	$74,186	$79,116	$80,825	$82,578	$84,614	$86,913
L2	$66,975	$74,920	$79,899	$81,626	$83,395	$85,452	$87,774

Source: Ann Arbor Education Association. A key to the abbreviations follows: "BA" means a bachelor's degree; "BA + 30" means a bachelor's degree and 30 credit-hours of additional coursework; "MA" means a master's degree; "MA + 30" means a master's degree and 30 credit-hours of additional coursework; "BA + 60W/MA" means a master's degree and a total of 60 credit-hours of coursework in addition to that required for a bachelor's degree; "2 MA" means two master's degrees; "ED. SPEC." means an "education specialist degree," which is effectively an intermediate degree between a master's degree and a Ph.D.; "BA + 90/MA" means a master's degree and a total of 90 credit-hours of coursework in addition to that required for a bachelor's degree; and "PH.D" means a doctorate.

Given that credentials and experience form the basis for teacher compensation across the state, it is worthwhile to evaluate whether these characteristics are associated with greater effectiveness in the classroom.

In studies that disaggregate various teacher characteristics, teacher experience is shown to impact student achievement positively, but only over the first few years of a teacher's career. By a teacher's fourth or fifth year, his or her effectiveness tends to be set. Effective teachers remain relatively effective, and ineffective teachers remain relatively ineffective.

Several studies support this conclusion. In the study of Alabama public schools cited earlier (see "A Teacher's Own Academic Ability"), Ferguson and Ladd determined that experience matters little after five years. They write, "[T]he teacher experience variable, teachers with five or more years of experience, apparently exerts no significant effect in either subject."[29]

Steven Rivkin, Eric Hanushek and John Kain include a similar finding in their study of teacher impacts on student achievement in Texas public schools during the 1990s. Rivkin, Hanushek and Kain write, "There appear to be important gains in teaching quality in the first year of experience and smaller gains over the next few career years. However, there is little evidence that improvements continue after the first three years."[30] These researchers also find that all beginning teachers — even those who will ultimately become quite effective — tend to be less effective than their more experienced counterparts.[31]

The only recent study that shows that veteran teachers with more than five years of experience become more effective in later stages of their careers is by Charles Clotfelter, Helen Ladd and Jacob Vigdor of Duke University. The primary purpose of their study was to examine whether students with socioeconomic advantages end up with better-qualified teachers.[32] Reviewing North Carolina achievement data for fifth-grade students, Clotfelter, Ladd and Vigdor presented findings indicating that highly experienced teachers were most successful at raising student achievement. All experienced teachers — even those with only one to two years of experience — were significantly more effective than novice teachers, but the "relationship between student achievement and teacher experience [was] nonlinear, with the peak occurring in those classrooms with teachers having between 13 and 26 years of experience; novice teachers (the omitted base category) [were] associated with the lowest test scores."[33] This same research team has also recently evaluated the impacts of teacher credentials on student achievement with high school students in North Carolina, and in this study, their findings were more consistent with the bulk of the research evidence concerning the role of teacher experience.[34] Clotfelter, Ladd and Vigdor again found that teachers with one to two years of experience were significantly more effective than novice teachers, but this time they are clear that highly experienced teachers, while also more effective than novice teachers, were not significantly more effective than those with one to two years.

Indeed, the weight of the evidence confirms Rivkin, Hanushek and Kain's findings.[35] In a study published by the nonprofit Center for Analysis of Longitudinal Data in Education Research, Dan Goldhaber found, "Students with a teacher who has one to two years of experience outperform students with novice teachers by 3 [percent] to 7 percent of a standard deviation, and students with teachers who have three to five years of experience tend to outperform those with one to two years of experience by an additional 2 percent of a standard deviation."[36] These differences are not particularly large, but they are informative when paired with Goldhaber's finding that there is "little evidence, however, of statistically significant productivity gains associated with increases in experience beyond five years."[37]

Jay Greene, chair of the Department of Education Reform at the University of Arkansas, suggests in his book "Education Myths" that teachers improve in the first few years because they get better at classroom management.[38] When teachers become more able to control groups of students, they can spend more time on instruction and less on discipline. In discussing the benefits of having experienced teachers, Greene also reports, "There is even some evidence that teachers get less effective in the later stages of their careers, perhaps because of the adverse incentives arising from the inability of most schools to fire veteran teachers even when their performance is very poor."[39]

The incentives created with teacher tenure and compensation policies are discussed later. For now, however, it is important to make clear that although experience may lead teachers to be more effective at certain points in their careers, each year of experience does not make a teacher commensurately more effective over the course of a career.

Master's Degrees

Research has also been conducted to determine whether master's degrees, which approximately 50 percent of all teachers hold, influence student achievement.[40] This question is particularly relevant to teacher compensation. The single salary schedule, which operates in more than 95 percent of districts nationwide, offers teachers significant pay raises for earning a master's degree.[41] As Dan Goldhaber has reported,

"[D]ata from the National Center for Education Statistics show that salary schedules provide pay premiums of about 11 percent for master's degrees and 17 percent for a doctorate."[42]

Despite the higher compensation provided to teachers with master's degrees, the bulk of the evidence shows that, in fact, master's degrees rarely appear to make teachers more effective.[xvii] Ferguson and Ladd found that master's degrees had a very small positive effect on student achievement in math, but not in reading. In their analysis of school level inputs, they write: "A one-standard deviation increase in the fraction of teachers with a master's degree (0.33 points) would increase student test scores by 0.026 standard deviations, about one-quarter of the effect of a standard deviation in teacher test scores."[xviii, 43]

Hanushek and colleagues have repeatedly found, "[A] master's degree has no systematic relationship to teacher quality as measured by student outcomes."[44] In his own study of teacher testing from 2006 (discussed below), Dan Goldhaber recently confirmed Hanushek's findings that master's degrees have little impact on teacher quality. Goldhaber wrote: "Consistent with much of the educational productivity literature (for example, Hanushek 1986, 1997), there is little evidence that a teacher having a master's degree (or higher) is a signal of teacher effectiveness."[45]

Goldhaber's 2002 summary of other research findings on master's degrees was somewhat more refined, however. He reported, "[T]he effect of degrees appears to hinge on the subjects that are taught and whether the degrees are specific to those subjects."[46] Goldhaber pointed to evidence that teachers with advanced coursework in math and science seem to be slightly more effective. He added, "Having an advanced degree in subjects outside of math and science, however, does not appear to affect student achievement."[47] Goldhaber did not

---

xvii Other studies that assert that master's degrees do not have a positive relationship with student outcomes include Donald Boyd et al., "The Effect of Certification and Preparation on Teacher Quality," *The Future of Children* 17, no. 1 (2007); Stotsky and Haverty, "Can a State Department of Education Increase Teacher Quality? Lessons Learned in Massachusetts"; Loeb and Reininger, "Public Policy and Teacher Labor Markets: What We Know and Why It Matters."

xviii The study did not appear to distinguish between the types of master's degrees, meaning that an MA, MS and MEd were considered equivalent and represented by one variable (as a proportion of the staff).

address whether the apparently higher achievement of teachers with advanced math and science degrees had been driven by self-selection bias — in other words, the possibility that the degrees did not improve the teachers' performance, but instead that highly effective math and science teachers tend to get subject-specific advanced degrees.

Until sophisticated "value-added" calculations entered mainstream education research during the last few years, high-quality studies on the impacts of advanced degrees on teacher effectiveness were in short supply.[xix] Nearly all recent research, however, suggests that master's degrees do not make for significantly better teachers.

Certification

In Michigan, all conventional public school teachers must be certified,[48] and nearly 99 percent of certified teachers in the state earn their certification through traditional means.[49] The No Child Left Behind Act also requires teachers to have state certification in order to earn the "highly qualified" teacher designation. Given that all teachers must meet this NCLB requirement, it is important to explore what is involved in earning certification in Michigan, to examine the rationale behind this quality-control mechanism, to determine whether certification affects student achievement and ultimately to explore whether there are ways to improve teacher quality by reforming the certification process.

Having a command of the subject and some experience as an instructor would not qualify a teacher to be certified in Michigan. Rather, a teacher must have at least a bachelor's degree from an accredited college or university and must complete coursework at an approved teacher preparation program.[xx] The hours of university coursework required to earn an endorsement in a given subject or grade level vary. According to the Michigan Teacher Certification Code, "'Certificate endorsement' means subject or subjects that a teacher is authorized to teach at specific grade levels based on completion of appropriate

---

xix These "value-added" calculations will be described in more detail in "Using Value-Added Assessment to Define Teacher Quality," Page 63.

xx Information about programs at approved teacher preparation institutions can be found at the Michigan Department of Education Office of Professional Preparation Services Web page on "Approved Teacher Preparation Programs," https://mdoe.state .mi.us/proprep/.

coursework and passage of the appropriate state teacher subject area examination."[50] To be certified, all teachers must pass at least two of the Michigan Test for Teacher Certification exams.[xxi, 51]

In Michigan, a teaching license is granted at completion of the certification process and is valid for five years.[52] The terms "teaching license" and "teaching certificate" are commonly used interchangeably. According to the Michigan Department of Education: "The renewal of a Professional Education certificate requires the completion of 6 semester hours of credit (these credits may be completed at a 2-year or 4-year institution) or 18 State Board-Continuing Education Units (SB-CEUs) or a combination of the two. Three SB-CEUs equals one semester hour. The required credit hours or SB-CEUs must be completed after the issuance of the Professional Education certificate and within five years of the date of application for the renewal."[53] For teachers who were trained or provisionally certified outside of Michigan, the procedures for earning or renewing a teaching certificate are also rather complicated.

The requirements for initial licensure vary somewhat based on the teacher preparation program. The state sets minimum standards for hours of coursework that constitute a major and minor, 30 and 20 hours respectively, but individual teacher preparation programs can choose to require additional training.[54] To earn an elementary provisional teaching certificate, a teacher must complete no fewer than six semester credit hours in teaching reading;[55] for the secondary provisional certificate, teachers must take at least three credit hours in teaching reading.[56] Aside from passing the testing requirements outlined in the next section, a final requirement for certification is that a teacher must participate in student teaching that is coordinated and supervised through an approved program.[57]

At the time of this writing, Michigan has 31 approved teacher preparation programs. Teacher preparation programs are approved by the State Board of Education when they meet the program standards articulated by the Michigan Department of Education and pass the review that is part of approval process. Preparation programs must also pass annual quality reviews by the MDE.

Pursuant to Title II of the U.S. Higher Education Act, the MDE

---

xxi   Teacher testing is discussed at length in the next section, "Performance on Teacher Licensing Exams," Page 39.

recently rated these programs. The MDE uses a 70-point scale: 40 points are earned through participant completion rates, the degree to which programs prepare teachers to fill high-demand slots, surveys of teacher candidates regarding their programs and the percentage of students taking the licensure exams who belong to minority groups. The final 30 points are based on a three-year aggregate of the specialty content area licensing exams.[xxii] The overall ratings are "exemplary," "satisfactory," "at-risk" or "low performing."[58]

In the 2007 report, which reported program performance in the 2005-2006 academic year, 18 programs were rated "exemplary." The two highest-scoring programs were at Oakland University and Hope College; each earned 68 total points. Andrews University, Eastern Michigan University, Grand Valley State University, Michigan State University and the University of Michigan-Dearborn tied for third, with a rating of 66 points. Ten programs earned a "satisfactory" rating, and one — Olivet — was rated "at-risk."[59] Finally, two of Michigan's teacher preparation programs — Adrian College and Marygrove College — were deemed "low performing," the lowest possible category. According to the MDE: "Institutions identified as low performing have two years to improve their performance before state sanctions occur. Institutions identified as at-risk must progress to the satisfactory category within two years or move to the low performing category, even if their raw score is still in the at-risk level."[xxiii, 60]

The stated purpose of requiring all teachers to become certified is to establish minimum standards for teacher quality, so qualified teacher

---

xxii   While federal law mandates that all states rate their teacher preparation programs annually, each state has discretion over the rating criteria it will use.

xxiii   According to the most recent data in a U.S. Secretary of Education report, 17 programs nationally fell into the remediation categories of "low performing" or "at-risk" in 2005. These national data on preparation programs show that 11 states had failing programs. Three states, Illinois, Kansas and South Carolina, each had three programs on the list. No Michigan colleges of education were rated in either category at that time (2002-2005), though the three listed above fall into those categories now. It is difficult to assess whether Michigan's relatively high rate of lower-performing teacher preparation programs is the result of truly underperforming institutions or of a tougher evaluation system. (See "The Secretary's Fifth Annual Report on Teacher Quality: A Highly Qualified Teacher in Every School Classroom," 141.) The same federal report also stated that at least 90 percent of Michigan's public school teachers graduated from Michigan colleges of education.

training experts have vouched that a new teacher has the requisite skills to be successful before that teacher takes charge of a classroom. Thus, teacher certification is theoretically akin to professional certification for doctors, lawyers and engineers.

Certification in these other fields, however, usually involves a much more rigorous screening and training process. As a result, the achievements of personnel who actually earn their certification in these other fields tend to be higher. If policymakers were to raise teacher certification requirements to sift out low-quality teaching candidates, they would need to change other features of the labor market to avoid negative unintended consequences. For example, simply raising the certification requirements could exacerbate shortages in high-needs areas, such as special education and secondary and middle school mathematics and science, since some candidates might not be willing (or able) to satisfy the expanded requirements. Moreover, since raising certification standards could require considerable legislative action, it is important to examine whether the quality of education is helped by extensive certification requirements.

Stanford's Linda Darling-Hammond, perhaps the most prominent advocate of teacher certification, released a study in 2005 with her colleagues in which she explored whether having traditional certification makes teachers more effective.[61] Darling-Hammond et al. analyzed fourth- and fifth-grade student achievement data from the Houston public schools from 1995 through 2002. They found that teachers with traditional certification were generally more effective at producing student achievement gains than those who were teaching without certification or who had become certified through alternative means. This finding included teachers from Teach for America, a program that offers limited teacher training to uncertified, academically able recent college graduates before placing them as teachers for two years in economically disadvantaged schools.[62] Other studies of Teach for America are discussed at length below.

In reporting her results, Darling-Hammond cited numerous studies with concurring opinions.[63] In a more recent study of North Carolina elementary school student achievement in 2007,[xxiv] Goldhaber

---

xxiv This study is discussed again in "Performance on Teacher Licensing Exams," Page 39.

finds, "[S]tudents of teachers who graduate from a North Carolina-approved training program outperform those whose teachers do not (that is, those who get a degree from an alternative state program or a program from outside the state) by about 1 percent of a standard deviation. ..."[64] Although this finding was statistically significant, it is difficult to argue that such a small difference has practical significance for policymakers.

The other side of this dispute is represented by equally prominent researchers — for example, Eric Hanushek — whose analyses show that certified teachers perform no better or worse than their uncertified colleagues.[65] Opponents of certification argue that certification erects unnecessary barriers to entry into the teaching profession, especially for career-changers.

Considerable evidence exists to support their claims. For example, in a recent, detailed study of New York City public school teachers, Thomas Kane of Harvard University, Jonah Rockoff of Columbia University and Douglas Staiger of Dartmouth College explored the relative effectiveness of teachers with traditional certification, alternative certification and no certification in New York City public schools.[66] As the authors explained, New York City schools are particularly interesting for the study of teacher certification because large numbers of the city's teachers fall into each certification category. Of the more than 50,000 new teachers hired in the district from 1999 through 2005, 46 percent were certified; 34 percent were uncertified; and 20 percent were alternatively certified. Most of the alternatively certified teachers participate in the New York City Teaching Fellows program,[67] in which they are given provisional certificates and intensive preservice teacher training. They also enroll in a master's degree program that will allow them to earn full certification upon completion of three successful years of teaching in the district.[68] Uncertified Teach for America teachers are also well represented, although they form a small percentage of New York's total new teacher work force.

In examining the math and reading learning gains of New York City students in grades three through eight, Kane and colleagues found that the differing teaching credentials produced minimal differences in student performance. The researchers found: "On average, the students assigned to [the alternatively certified] teaching fellows performed similarly to students assigned to certified teachers in math, and slightly lower (-.01 standard deviations) in reading. ... We find evidence that Teach for America corps members have slightly higher value-added (.02 standard deviations) for math test scores than traditionally certified teachers, but we find no difference in reading."[69]

Kane, Rockoff and Staiger's findings are similar to those of the Mathematica Policy Research's study of Teach for America teachers. In this study, Mathematica used a random assignment experimental research design to measure the effectiveness of TFA participants compared to teachers with traditional credentials.[70] Randomized design is the gold standard of social science research, and the findings of such experiments are usually given extra weight.[xxv, 71]

In the Mathematica study, students in 17 schools representing six geographically diverse regions of the country were randomly assigned to certified teachers or uncertified TFA teachers. The researchers found that students of TFA teachers demonstrated more growth in math than those of their certified peers, while students of TFA teachers did not routinely score any differently from other students in reading. As the authors of this study point out, their findings help to settle the dispute that has resulted from the mixed findings on the effectiveness of TFA in quasi-experimental research designs.[xxvi]

---

xxv Randomized experimental designs, also known as randomized controlled trials or randomized field trials, are experiments in which participants subjected to a given treatment are selected for that treatment essentially by a flip of the coin. In these experiments, those who are not selected for the treatment are placed into a control group for the sake of comparison. Because participants in the experiment are placed in the treatment and control groups simply by chance, this randomization distributes variation in study participants' characteristics equally between the two groups. As a result, researchers can be confident that any differences in the groups after the treatment occurs are due to the treatment and not to any pre-existing differences in the two groups. The primary alternative social science methodology to random assignment studies is called "quasi-experimental research," which involves significant statistical controls. This quasi-experimental research predominates in education studies for many reasons, while random assignment experimental research is exceedingly rare. (See Thomas D. Cook, "Considering the Major Arguments Against Random Assignment: An Analysis of the Intellectual Culture Surrounding Evaluation in American Schools of Education," *Harvard Faculty Seminar on Experiments in Education* (Cambridge, Mass.: 1999).)
xxvi Summarizing the mixed research literature on Teach for America instructors prior to the Mathematica study, Decker, Mayer and Glazerman wrote: "Despite TFA's rapid expansion, there is little evidence whether teachers with strong academic

Two other reforms related to raising certification requirements could also be considered. First, compensation levels and methods could be enhanced to motivate potential teachers to accept the opportunity costs involved in earning a more rigorous certification. Alternatively, since research suggests that traditional certification is not a guarantee of teacher quality, policymakers could remove some certification requirements that may act more as a deterrent to potential teachers than as a guarantee of quality. University coursework in pedagogy, for instance, has not been shown to improve teacher performance.

---

backgrounds, but limited exposure to teaching practice, can be effective. Some critics argue that programs such as TFA are 'loopholes' that permit unlicensed and under-trained teachers into the classroom simply as a way to address teacher shortages. Darling-Hammond (1994, 1996) has argued that TFA teachers 'often have difficulty with curriculum development, pedagogical content knowledge, students' different learning styles, classroom management, and student motivation.' Other researchers are more optimistic about the potential benefits of hiring teachers through programs such as TFA. Ballou and Podgursky (1998) argue that there is no evidence that formal teacher certification produces more qualified teachers and that certification policies may discourage talented individuals from entering the profession. Two recent studies (Raymond et al. 2001, and Laczko-Kerr and Berliner 2002) attempted to assess the impact of TFA using nonexperimental methods on samples drawn from single regions, and generated mixed findings regarding the effectiveness of TFA teachers." (Decker, Mayer and Glazerman, "The Effects of Teach for America on Students." See also Raymond, Fletcher and Luque, "Teach for America: An Evaluation of Teacher Differences and Student Outcomes in Houston, Texas" and Ildiko Laczko-Kerr and David C. Berliner, "The Effectiveness of 'Teach for America' and Other Under-certified Teachers on Student Academic Achievement: A Case of Harmful Public Policy," *Education Policy Analysis Archives*, 10, no. 37 (2002).)

Note that the study by Darling-Hammond et al. of the Houston public schools used a quasi-experimental design. In that report, Darling-Hammond criticized this Mathematica study, arguing that it did not choose an appropriate control group. Even bearing her criticism in mind, the Mathematica study is a particularly strong data point questioning the contention that traditional teacher certification is necessary for student success.

One other objection might be raised against the studies cited in this section: They do not involve certified teachers in Michigan. Since states have different certification requirements, it might be argued that Michigan has a superior certification process that would in fact be linked to teacher effectiveness in an unbiased study. Such an outcome is unlikely, however. The studies cited in this section are among the highest-quality in the field, and there is no reason to believe that Michigan's teaching corps and teacher preparation programs are dramatically different from the other states studied.

By making such coursework elective, rather than required, Michigan might be able to attract new teachers who would be at least as effective as those currently in the profession.[xxvii]

Performance on Teacher Licensing Exams

As noted in the previous section, teachers wishing to obtain licensure in the state of Michigan must pass the Michigan Test for Teacher Certification. Given some of the questions raised about the value of certification, it is important to explore whether teacher testing alone, as opposed to certification as it currently exists, might be a viable teacher quality reform.

According to Pearson Education Inc., the company which produces the MTTC through its affiliate National Evaluation Systems Inc., "The purpose of the [MTTC] tests is to ensure that each certified teacher has the necessary basic skills and content knowledge to serve in Michigan public schools."[72] The tests are tailored specifically to Michigan state teacher preparation standards and administered by NES, an independent contractor located in Amherst, Mass. The MTTC exams are criterion-referenced, rather than norm-referenced, meaning that teacher candidates are measured against a set of standards, not against each other.

To become certified in Michigan, teacher candidates must pass two MTTC exams.[73] All teaching candidates must pass a basic skills test, which has subtests in math, reading and writing, before student teaching; some teacher preparation programs require that teacher candidates pass the basic skills test even before enrolling. Elementary school teachers (kindergarten through fifth grade) must also pass the MTTC Elementary Education test. Secondary school teachers (grades six through 12) must pass an MTTC subject area test in their chosen

---

xxvii   As Goldhaber has written: "If the required credentials are only weakly correlated with student achievement, it will result in significant numbers of 'false positives' and 'false negatives' — that is, many applicants who satisfy the criteria for employment eligibility turn out to be ineffective teachers (false positives), and many who do not satisfy the criteria but who would have been effective in the classroom had they been allowed into the teacher workforce (false negatives). The false negatives may never persevere to become teachers — a loss to the profession — and the false positives may be difficult to remove from the classroom once they have attained the job security, via tenure, which typically exists in public schools." See Goldhaber, "Teacher Pay Reforms," 6.

field of instruction, although middle school teachers (grades six through eight) must pass the MTTC Elementary Education test instead if they teach in "self-contained classrooms," in which a single teacher teaches all subjects.[74]

More than 10 states, including Michigan, use NES tests as a part of their certification process (other states use the Praxis series of tests, which are administered by the Educational Testing Service, a competing company). Each state determines its own passing scores. Citing Ruth Mitchell and Patte Barth of the nonprofit Education Trust, Sandra Stotsky of the University of Arkansas' Department of Education Reform has reported that over 50 percent of new teachers are licensed in states that use NES tests.[75] She has also noted, "There are no data across states on how many test items need to be correct for a passing score on each of the different tests that states require."[76]

The federal government collects information on state certification test passage rates both for the basic skills and subject area tests. According to the most recent federal data, Michigan is one of four states to report a 100 percent passage rate on content area tests and one of six states to report a 100 percent passage rate on basic skills tests.[77] These are not the passage rates for every teacher candidate taking the tests, however; instead, they are the passage rates for provisionally certified teachers. Since all teachers are required to pass the MTTC basic skills and content area tests before becoming provisionally certified, the passage rates are essentially 100 percent by definition.[xxviii, 78]

Not surprisingly, however, the MTTC passage rates for teaching *candidates* are typically less than 100 percent and differ among teacher preparation programs. The best available data for comparing the state's teacher preparation programs on the MTTC exams are the specialty content area test scores, since at many colleges, students are not permitted to enter teacher preparation programs if they have not already passed the basic skills. Graphic 8, adapted from a 2006 report by State Superintendent of Public Instruction Michael P. Flanagan, shows

---

xxviii   Federal data actually show a few more people taking the exams than passing them, but the difference is negligible (much less than 1 percent; hence, the 100 percent pass rate after rounding). The reason for the discrepancy is unclear. (See "The Secretary's Fifth Annual Report on Teacher Quality: A Highly Qualified Teacher in Every School Classroom.")

a three-year aggregate of teaching candidates' passage rates on MTTC specialty content exams. In comparing the schools, the MDE confers a "summary score" on each institution based upon the pass rate: 30 points for 90 percent or higher; 25 points for 85 percent to 89.9 percent; 20 points for 80 percent to 84.9 percent; and zero points for less than 80 percent.[79] These summary scores also appear in Graphic 8.

Graphic 8: Passage Rates for Teaching Candidates in Michigan Teacher Preparation Programs on Michigan Test for Teacher Certification Specialty Area Exams (Academic Year 2005-2006)

Teacher Preparation Program	Three-Year Aggregate of MTTC Specialty Passage Rates	MDE Summary Score
Calvin College	98	30
University of Michigan (Ann Arbor)	98	30
Michigan State University	97	30
Aquinas College	96	30
Grand Valley State University	96	30
Hope College	96	30
Northern Michigan University	95	30
Central Michigan University	94	30
Concordia University	94	30
Madonna University	94	30
Eastern Michigan University	93	30
Hillsdale College	93	30
Oakland University	93	30
Michigan Technological University	92	30
Cornerstone University	92	30
Alma College	91	30
Saginaw Valley State University	91	30
Andrews University	90	30
Spring Arbor University	90	30
University of Michigan-Dearborn	90	30
Wayne State University	90	30
Albion College	90	30
Ferris State University	90	30
Western Michigan University	90	30
University of Michigan-Flint	89	25
Olivet Nazarene University	89	25
Lake Superior State University	88	25
Siena Heights University	86	25
Adrian College	84	20
University of Detroit Mercy	80	20
Marygrove College	65	0

Sources: Michigan Department of Education

Unfortunately, teacher licensure tests may not actually be measuring knowledge that makes teachers effective. Stotsky reviewed three different Michigan licensure tests to determine whether they credibly evaluated understanding of reading pedagogy: the tests taken by general elementary school teachers, by building-level reading specialists and by elementary teachers with a specific endorsement in reading. Specifically, Stotsky sought to identify the presence of questions measuring phonemic awareness, phonics and vocabulary knowledge — "three of the basic components of beginning reading instruction ... each of which is supported by a large, consistent, and credible body of research evidence."[80]

Her assessment is not encouraging. She found that critical reading instruction knowledge areas were tested by only 2 percent, 4 percent and 5 percent of the items on the Michigan licensure tests for general elementary school teachers, building-level reading specialists and elementary teachers with a specific endorsement in reading, respectively.

Stotsky also compared the content of NES tests, such as those used in Michigan, and ETS tests. Distinguishing between the two is important: NES tests are tailored specifically to a state's requests and therefore reflect the wishes of state education officials, while ETS tests have standard content. Stotsky concluded that states using NES tests tended to focus more on important reading content knowledge than those using ETS tests, but she added: "[A]t least two NES states (Michigan and Illinois) have no higher expectations than those states using ETS's elementary tests. A state gets what it asks for if it uses NES."[81]

Given that all teachers in the state must pass at least two tests, several questions arise as to whether teacher testing has a positive influence on work force quality. For example, do teachers who perform better on these tests perform better in the classroom? Would requiring higher cut scores on these exams help to create a better teaching corps? Alternatively, should we do away with teacher testing altogether? The existing research provides guidance on some of these questions.

In a study mentioned earlier (see Page 29), Clotfelter, Ladd and Vigdor of Duke University examined North Carolina data and explored questions regarding teacher performance on licensure tests.[82] They found: "Students assigned to teachers with higher licensure test scores apparently do better in math, but the effect is relatively modest.

A one-standard deviation increase in teacher test score implies at most a 0.017 standard deviation increase in average student math test scores and a somewhat smaller increase in reading scores."[83] In other words, they found that students who have teachers who score at the 85th percentile on licensure tests tend to do slightly better in math and reading than students with teachers who score at the 50th percentile. These researchers attribute much of this difference to their finding that students with socioeconomic advantages tend to attend schools with higher-scoring teachers. This conclusion would suggest that the value of a higher-scoring teacher may be even smaller than Clotfelter and colleagues calculated.

In a recent study of teacher testing, Dan Goldhaber, whose other findings are reported above, explored many of the relevant questions about teacher testing with high-quality empirical analysis.[84] Goldhaber used a North Carolina data set that relates teachers to individual student test scores on standardized achievement tests. In 1997, the North Carolina set passage cut points on ETS Praxis exams, but in 2000, the state raised them. Goldhaber found that fourth- through sixth-grade teachers who would have passed even under the new cut scores were slightly more effective in promoting student achievement in math: Their students outperformed the students of teachers who would not have passed by 6 percent of a standard deviation.

Then Goldhaber studied the potential effect of even higher cut points to see how they would have affected the North Carolina teacher labor market. Goldhaber borrowed the cut point set by Connecticut, a state which uses a similar set of teacher tests. Interestingly, he discovered that using Connecticut's higher cut point would have prevented many North Carolina teachers who were actually more effective than their higher-scoring peers from entering the classroom.

Finally, Goldhaber examined whether there is a relatively linear relationship between higher teacher test performance and higher student test performance. He found that teachers who score in the top 20 percent of test takers are more effective in promoting student achievement than those who score in the bottom 20 percent, but that the magnitude of the difference is not particularly large. The conclusions of his study are that teachers who score higher on teacher licensure tests may be slightly more effective, but that teacher testing may exclude some potential teachers who would ultimately turn out to be more effective.[85]

Thus, the research suggests that teachers who score better on licensure tests generally are more effective than those who score less well. Still, the gains from having a teacher who scores well are fairly small in math and even smaller in reading. Moreover, the fact that a teacher scores exceptionally well does not guarantee quality, and to the extent that teacher testing forms a barrier to entry for teachers who might turn out to be effective, testing is not a particularly helpful quality-control mechanism. There are also many practical difficulties (which Stotsky pointed out[86]) involved in raising cut scores appropriately, and the value of doing so is further limited to the extent that higher cut scores exacerbate teacher labor shortages in high-demand fields. At best, testing may be one basic signal of teacher competence, but policymakers should be careful when interpreting gradations in teacher test scores.

Part IV: The Context of Teacher Quality Reforms

If research on teacher quality suggests that certain characteristics tend to make teachers more effective, the reasonable question is, What reforms can Michigan policymakers use to encourage teachers with those characteristics to join and to remain in the teaching work force? Under the current compensation system, experience and credentials are rewarded. However, as shown in the previous section, the assumptions that these characteristics are related to teacher effectiveness have generally been rendered doubtful by academic research. If policymakers want to improve teacher quality, they should consider policy solutions that will change the current incentive structure and maximize teachers' effectiveness in the classroom.

Specifically, policymakers need to think about how to recruit new teachers who have a greater potential for success; encourage the retention of teachers who have proven that they can raise student achievement; weed out teachers who have been unable or unwilling to raise student achievement; and motivate formerly effective teachers who are not achieving their potential. In this section, I review and recommend incentive-based policies to improve teacher quality. First, however, I examine two often-discussed alternative educational reforms that operate on different principles.

Across-the-Board Salary Increases

One strategy for improving teacher quality in the state that is commonly advocated by teachers unions, such as the Michigan Education Association, is across-the-board teacher pay raises. Proponents of this strategy argue that higher wages would draw higher-performing undergraduates into teaching. Advocates also claim that such pay hikes would address teacher supply shortages by encouraging workers in other fields to shift to teaching and by motivating teachers who have decided to stay at home to reactivate their careers.

Dale Ballou and Michael Podgursky have considered whether across-the-board pay raises would increase the quality of teachers by attracting a larger pool of higher-quality applicants to the profession.[87] Using academic ability as their measure of teacher quality, these researchers use a complicated equation from the field of labor economics to estimate that the likely effect on teacher quality of "a 20% raise — equal to the increase in real salaries over the 1980s — is not encouraging. Under plausible assumptions about teacher behavior, [the] average cognitive ability [of the teacher population would remain] below the mean for the college educated population."[88]

They argue that several unintended negative consequences would likely result from such a reform. First, higher salaries would encourage older, already more expensive teachers, to remain on the job longer. This retention of older teachers would prevent the entry of many new higher-quality teachers attracted by the higher salary. Second, higher salaries without increases to the overall budget would quickly lead to layoffs, which would differentially affect newer hires. Ballou and Podgursky explain that such an unintended consequence undermines the whole point of offering higher wages to teachers in the first place, since the promising, newly hired teachers would be the first to be squeezed out. A third unintended consequence is that higher-quality applicants who are considering other career options would actually be deterred from teaching as the probability of obtaining a job offer falls with increased competition from higher numbers of applicants.

Writing for Michigan State University's Education Policy Center, Susanna Loeb and Michelle Reininger offered yet another unintended consequence of a policy of substantial across-the-board raises. They explain that such a policy would lead to wasting limited resources to increase salaries in high-supply fields, such as elementary school teachers or physical education teachers. [89]

Raising teacher salaries will not only have unintended consequences; it is also unwarranted in Michigan. National Education Association President Reg Weaver recently wrote that increasing the salaries of all teachers to make them "competitive with other professions that require a college degree" would be a way to use compensation to improve teacher quality.[90] Perhaps teacher salaries are low compared to those of other degreed professions in some parts of the country, and attracting quality teachers to hard-to-staff areas of the state may well require a compensating differential in pay.[xxix] Nonetheless, it is hard to argue that across-the-board salary increases should come to Michigan, where the most recent estimates by the federal Bureau of Labor Statistics place the average elementary school teacher salary (not including special

---

xxix   As discussed later, attracting teachers to hard-to-staff fields, such as upper-level math and science, may require higher salaries, too.

education teachers) at $56,170 in 2007. National Education Association estimates place this average salary figure even higher at $58,482.[91] Graphic 9 shows the average 2007 salaries of workers in Michigan in professions that require college degrees. These figures are actual salary averages; they have not been annualized. In other words, they have not been adjusted to reflect that teachers work fewer days annually on average than many of the other professions listed below. The occupations chosen for comparison are those that require at least a four-year degree and that have workers who often earn advanced degrees.

Graphic 9: 2007 Average Salaries in Michigan for Professions Requiring College Degrees

Occupation	Salary
Registered Nurses	$61,030
Accountants and Auditors	$61,020
Biological Scientists	$58,380
Elementary Teachers	$56,170
Writers and Authors	$54,860
Secondary School Teachers	$54,560
Public Relations Specialists	$54,060
Historians	$50,240
Child, Family, School Social Workers	$49,450
Mental Health Counselors	$44,090

Source: U.S. Bureau of Labor Statistics. Biological scientists do not include zoologists and wildlife biologists. Elementary school teachers exclude special education teachers, and secondary school teachers exclude both special and vocational education teachers.

Teacher salaries are the largest single expense in education budgets, and it is true that dramatically increasing the education budget at state and local levels would enable schools to pay teachers higher salaries across the board. However, there is no reason to believe that such a reform would make teachers any more effective. As demonstrated in Part I, Michigan's generous increases in educational spending, which have also included across-the-board salary increases for teachers, have not resulted in commensurate improvements in student achievement.

It could, however, be argued that even larger across-the-board increases would likely attract higher-quality undergraduates and more career-changers to the field. Such a strategy ignores budgetary constraints. In light of the state government's real spending difficulties,[92] advocating large and uniform teacher pay increases to address substandard student achievement seems neither a realistic nor an efficient solution.

Policymakers should begin to consider alternatives to the norms that have traditionally guided primary and secondary public education. Rather than spending more money, the goal should be to choose the systemic reforms that are most likely to bring about improvements in student outcomes with the money available. Reapportioning the vast sums of money already set aside for public education by changing how money is spent can alter the incentives for teachers in ways that will effect positive change, and that notion should begin to guide education policymakers at state and local levels. In their discussions during education committee meetings and school board meetings, policymakers will have to address a popular alternative to market-based teacher quality reforms — class-size reductions.

Class-Size Reductions

Commonly advocated by groups like the MEA, class-size reductions are aimed at improving teacher effectiveness by allowing teachers to focus on a smaller number of students. Teachers would have fewer papers to grade, questions to answer, behavior problems to manage and parents to consult; as a result, individual students would get more attention, learn more and improve their achievement.

In a September 2007 letter to The New York Times, the NEA's Reg Weaver clarified the union's position on student-teacher ratios when he stated that the federal government needs to "provide resources for programs that improve test scores, such as smaller class sizes. ..."[93] In support of a federal class-size reduction program, President Bill Clinton said: "Reducing class size is one of the most important investments we can make in our children's future. Recent research confirms what parents have always known — children learn better in small classes with good teachers, and kids who start out in smaller classes do better right through their high school graduation."[94]

Lowering class sizes does have intuitive appeal as a solution for low-performing schools. In a meticulous paper on class-size policies, Douglas Harris of the University of Wisconsin reported on survey results indicating that parents and the general public overwhelmingly support the idea of class-size reductions.[95] Harris explained that extensive class-size reductions passed as a referendum in Florida even in the face of resistance from the state's governor and of the general understanding that higher taxes would be needed to pay for the reform. He suggests that "one explanation for the popularity of small classes is that parents cannot easily observe many forms of educational quality."[96] Thus, he theorizes that parents may support class-size reduction policies because they are tangible reforms that can be enacted quickly.

Unfortunately, as Harris notes, class-size reduction may not be all that meets the eye. In a recent study of Texas student performance, Rivkin, Hanushek and Kain found that fourth- and fifth-grade students in smaller classes performed better in both math and reading. The effects of smaller classes got smaller each year, however, and were not apparent in grade seven.[97] Nonetheless, these researchers do not advocate class-size reductions as a policy solution to low student performance. Instead, they focus on improving teacher quality. They explain that improving teacher quality by one standard deviation — i.e. getting a teacher who ranks in quality at the 85th percentile rather than at the 50th percentile — "is equivalent to a class size reduction of approximately ten students in 4th grade and thirteen or more students in 5th grade, and an implausibly large number in 6th grade."[98]

A randomized experiment of lowering class sizes during the 1980s in Tennessee — the famous Tennessee STAR project — also showed that lowering class sizes in early elementary grades raised student achievement.[99] In this study, students were randomly assigned to three types of classrooms. The classroom ratios were 13-17 students to one teacher, 22-25 students to one teacher, and 22-25 students to one teacher and a teacher's aide. Aside from potential shortcomings in the study itself,[xxx] several unintended consequences prevent this strategy from becoming a feasible solution in Michigan. As Rivkin, Hanushek and

xxx For a discussion of the potential shortcomings in the Tennessee STAR study, see Greene, *Education Myths: What Special-Interest Groups Want You to Believe About Our Schools — and Why It Isn't So.*

Kain note, the costs associated with class-size reductions do not simply result from the costs of hiring additional teachers.[100] The need for extra classroom space and for more support staff cannot be ignored.

Perhaps the largest barrier to this reform is that the supply of high-quality teachers is limited, so the prospective gains from smaller student-to-teacher ratios would likely be undermined by staffing those classrooms with less effective teachers.[101] As Jay Greene writes in his book "Education Myths," "Even if class size reduction does produce improved performance under optimal conditions of a small, controlled experiment like the STAR project, labor pool problems may prevent this success from being reproduced on a large scale."[102] In other words, under class-size reduction policies, schools would be forced to hire more teachers, and those applicants may be the inferior teachers who were passed over in prior years.

In fact, this harmful substitution occurred during the late 1990s when California attempted widespread class-size reductions based partly on the perceived success of the Tennessee STAR experiment. California lowered the average number of students in a class from 28 to 20 in a program involving more than 1.8 million students, in contrast to the roughly 11,000 in Tennessee. The price tag was over $1.5 billion per year.[103] Although some third-grade students showed slight achievement gains, other reforms undertaken simultaneously in California at that time make it difficult to attribute these minimal gains to the class-size reduction policy. Moreover, even if class-size were responsible, the performance gains were meager given the cost.

The California program's evaluators were analysts from RAND Corp. and other leading research firms. Their report confirmed that principals had hired teachers of lower quality when the project was implemented.[104] The evaluators found: "While [the project] was being implemented, the qualifications of California's teacher work force declined. The proportion of teachers with full credentials decreased in all grades, ... as did the proportion of teachers with the minimum level of college education (only a bachelor's degree) and the proportion of experienced teachers (those with more than three years of experience)."[105] Even though these metrics for judging teacher quality are questionable, it is still safe to say that the quality of California's teaching work force declined.

The California program evaluators also reported that the class-size reduction project did not close the achievement gap between white and minority students and that schools serving disadvantaged students were the most likely to hire teachers with less desirable credentials.[106] Thus, California's class-size reduction policy was likely a failure, due at least in part to the low quality of additional teachers.[107] Given that the project cost $1.5 billion dollars relative to a total state education budget of $34.9 billion,[108] the modest and nonuniform gains simply did not justify the expense.

Although they were critical of California's program, B.J. Biddle and David Berliner of the East Lansing-based Great Lakes Center for Education Research & Practice are supporters of class-size reduction. Regarding California, they suggest that lowering class sizes only to 20 students was not sufficient to realize significant gains.[109] They also argue that there was not enough money to support the reform, and that, "[T]his inadequate funding imposed serious consequences on poorer school districts, which had to abolish other needed activities to afford hiring teachers for smaller classes."[110]

Yet simply increasing the budget for education is no trivial undertaking, and working within the reality of budgetary constraints, policymakers should consider the trade-offs involved with class-size reduction policies. As Jay Greene notes: "Any serious reduction in class sizes would require us to invest a very large amount of money, so we could only produce small classes by taking resources away from other educational priorities. ... Smaller classes would almost certainly leave insufficient funds left over for other, much more promising reform strategies. Success in reducing class sizes would be a Pyrrhic victory — more would ultimately be lost than gained."[111]

The cost of this trade-off is real, no matter what policies one prefers. The University of Wisconsin's Douglas Harris notes, "Resources that go to small classes and small schools cannot be used to buy laptops for teachers, raise teacher salaries, increase professional development, add pre-kindergarten programs, or purchase new textbooks."[xxxi, 112]

---

xxxi Research does not generally suggest that the alternative programs Harris mentions have a significant impact on student achievement. Nevertheless, Harris' point remains: Costly class-size reduction initiatives inevitably drain resources from other possible reforms.

Harris also provides a helpful guide for evaluating the costs and benefits of an education policy. He describes three ways to consider trade-offs: cost-benefit analysis, cost-effectiveness analysis and an "optimization" approach. Cost-benefit analysis is the most straightforward approach; it monetizes total costs and benefits and subtracts the former from the latter to determine the viability of a policy proposal. Cost-effectiveness analysis involves dividing incremental benefits by incremental costs, where incremental costs and benefits are the costs and benefits that accrue when looking at the next unit in a series. (The term "incremental" is equivalent to the economics term "marginal.") The higher the ratio of incremental benefits to incremental costs, the better the solution. The reason that cost-effectiveness analysis is helpful is because it allows us to compare the efficiency of multiple policy proposals even when the total costs and benefits of those proposals are of very different sizes.[113]

The optimization approach improves upon cost-effectiveness by considering the concept of diminishing marginal returns. In the optimization approach, the incremental costs and benefits are not assumed to be linear — or constant for each new unit — as they are in the cost-effectiveness analysis. In other words, as Harris explains, the incremental benefit of reducing a class size from 23 students to 22 students is not assumed to be the same as reducing the class size from three students to two students, for example. Under the optimization approach, the ratios that are calculated will point to the most cost-effective solution for class-size reduction by signaling the point at which reducing the class size by one more student is not as cost effective as the prior one-student reduction.[114]

Without any budgetary constraints, Harris explains, the optimization approach would be the most helpful. However, since budget constraints do exist, and since these can easily preclude achieving the optimal solution, the cost-effectiveness approach, even though it assumes linear costs and benefits, is preferable.

Harris reports on his earlier analysis, which "suggests that increasing test scores by 0.05 of a standard deviation by reducing class size would require $1,287 in additional expenditures per pupil, much more than the apparent $163 cost per pupil of achieving the same test score increase through an increase in teacher salaries."[115] According to Harris, his own findings are consistent with earlier research that he claims "suggest[s] that the broad-based trend toward smaller classes in recent decades has probably resulted in lower student achievement than would have been possible if other uses had been made of the resources available."[116] Harris is careful, however, to qualify his claims. He asserts that since incremental costs are in fact not linear, there may be situations where class-size reductions would be warranted. For example, Harris states that moving from an exceptionally large class may be a good idea. Still, Michigan's student-teacher ratios do not suggest extremely large class sizes. According to NEA estimates, the average student-teacher ratio during the 2004-2005 school year in Michigan was 17.8 students per teacher, compared to the national average of 15.8.[117] In 2007, the average student-teacher ratio in Michigan was down to 17.4 students per class.[xxxii, 118] The incremental gain to be captured by reducing student-teacher ratios by one or two students to get to the national average — i.e., moving from approximately 17.8 to 15.8 — would probably not be cost-effective.

Harris has made a comparison of the resources involved in increasing teacher salaries and decreasing class sizes. As shown earlier, across-the-board salary increases are not a particularly compelling solution. Harris's comparison is most helpful in demonstrating that class-size reductions, though popular, contain hidden costs. His calculations give some indication of the magnitude of costs associated with class-size reductions and lend support to the arguments of those who advocate looking at policy proposals from all angles.

One parting thought on class-size reductions: Policymakers should also recall that self-interest may be involved when teacher unions advocate class-size reduction policies. Terry Moe suggests that teachers unions support class-size reductions because they want more teachers, who in turn will become fee-payers or union members.[119] Douglas Harris disagrees with this notion, but argues that since class-size reduction policies are extremely popular among teachers, unions are simply

---

xxxii The NEA correctly notes that student-teacher ratio is not the same as average class size, but they do concede that "no state-by-state 'actual' class-size information exists." See "Class Size - NEA's Efforts to Gather Accurate Class Size Data," National Education Association, http://www.nea.org/classsize/datacollection.html (accessed May 17, 2008).

"representing the wishes of their members."[120] Perhaps Harris is right, but satisfying these wishes may not improve student achievement, even if they make teachers happier.

The point to take from this extended discussion of class-size reductions is that once again, the research suggests that policymakers should focus on ways to increase the number of highly effective teachers in the schools. As Jay Greene notes, students will do better in a larger class with a great teacher than they will do in a smaller class with an average or below-average teacher. [121]

Part V: Improving the Teacher Work Force Through Better Assessment

As discussed in previous sections, education research suggests that academic ability and verbal ability (and perhaps advanced degrees in math and science) are typical of effective teachers. Certification, extensive pedagogical training, master's degrees in education and experience after the first few years are inconsistent indicators at best. Clearly, these findings suggest that many of the incentive structures that motivate teachers to seek certain credentials and that encourage individuals to stay in the profession regardless of their classroom performance are misaligned. But does this mean that we should simply modify those practices to favor teachers with higher academic and verbal ability?

Probably not. While there may be some basis for thinking of such direct reforms, we must always remember the potential for a reform to have unintended consequences. As Goldhaber's research in North Carolina suggested (see Page 35), raising cut scores on teacher exams — one sign of a teacher's academic ability — can quickly start to exclude effective teachers. Moreover, we must remember that correlation is not causation. A high IQ does not always help a teacher be more effective in the classroom. After all, a particle physicist may struggle to explain elementary mechanics to students. By defining teacher quality in terms of growth in student achievement — the ultimate goal of policy reform — policymakers can focus on retaining and rewarding the teachers who help students succeed, not on teachers who only *might* be more effective.

Current Assessment Techniques

The federal No Child Left Behind Act of 2001 "requires that all teachers of core academic subjects in the classroom be highly qualified. This is determined by three essential criteria: (1) attaining a bachelor's degree or better in the subject taught; (2) obtaining full state teacher certification; and (3) demonstrating knowledge in the subjects taught."[122] NCLB allows states to determine the requirements that teachers must satisfy to become fully certified and to demonstrate knowledge in the subjects taught. Essentially, if Michigan teachers have gone through an approved teacher-training program and passed their licensure tests, they are considered highly qualified.[xxxiii] For veteran teachers who

---

xxxiii According to "Frequently Asked Questions for MTTC": "Generally, elementary and secondary teachers who have taken and passed MTTC tests in the subject-areas and

entered the classroom before NCLB and might not have met the general requirements, NCLB provided alternative ways for states to certify that such teachers were highly qualified.[xxxiv]

instructional levels in the classrooms for which they hold endorsement and to which they are assigned to teach, meet the NCLB highly qualified definition. Also, middle and secondary (grades 6-12) teachers who are assigned to teach in their academic majors, but may not have taken MTTC tests, are considered highly qualified. Elementary and secondary teachers assigned to middle grade or higher classrooms based on their minor subject-area endorsements, or on endorsements for which they have completed course credits that are equivalent to a minor, will be considered highly qualified AFTER they pass the MTTC test that corresponds to the subject-area and instructional level of the classroom in which they teach. Passing a MTTC test does NOT substitute for earning an endorsement in a subject-area." (Emphasis in original.)

xxxiv These alternative methods are known as "High Objective Uniform State Standards of Evaluation," or "HOUSSE." According to the "NCLB Revised Highly Qualified Teacher State Plan" (Michigan Department of Education, 2006), http://www.ed.gov/programs/teacherqual/hqtplans/mi.doc (accessed May 18, 2008): "The Michigan Department of Education has begun to phase out the uses of HOUSSE options. From the beginning, these options were available only to the previously identified groups of veteran Michigan teachers who were authorized by the state to teach a particular subject. As a point of clarification, veteran teachers employed prior to January 8, 2002 were the only teachers eligible to elect to use HOUSSE options. It is only the sub-group of veteran teachers facing reassignment due to downsizing of staff, who may select HOUSSE options in the future. All teachers currently employed must [have completed] their HOUSSE option by the June 30, 2006 deadline or prior to placement in the classroom for the 2006-2007 school year. Those teachers who [were] still eligible for the HOUSSE options [had] until June 30, 2007 to complete one of these options. After June 30, 2007 these teachers must either complete the equivalent of a major or take the Michigan Test for Teacher Certification (MTTC) in the specific subject areas for which they are authorized to teach but do not hold a major. No teacher can be considered Highly Qualified in Michigan unless he or she holds the appropriate certificate and endorsement for the subject. While NCLB provides flexibility for rural teachers to teach multiple subjects upon completion of a HOUSSE option and be considered Highly Qualified, Michigan law prohibits the teacher from doing so unless she or he holds the appropriate endorsement."

In a report on NCLB and HOUSSE, Kate Walsh and Emma Snyder indicated NCLB's HOUSSE provisions were not well-conceived (see Walsh and Snyder, "Searching the Attic: How States Are Responding to the Nation's Goal of Placing a Highly Qualified Teacher in Every Classroom" (National Council on Teacher Quality, 2004), http://www.nctq.org/nctq/images/housse_report_2.pdf (accessed May 18, 2008)). They describe how individual states were free to set the criteria of their HOUSSE plans, and many such plans allowed teachers to apply previously completed workshops, committee work or mentoring experiences to earn highly qualified status. It is from these provisions that their report got its title, for the image arises of teachers searching through their attics to find anything that would satisfy the HOUSSE plan.

Although NCLB is right to focus on teacher quality as an essential component of accountability, the law's "Highly Qualified Teacher" mechanism misses the mark. If the federal government is going to be involved in guiding state policy regarding teacher quality, the policy should focus on "Highly Effective Teachers," not "Highly Qualified Teachers."[xxxv] This distinction is not merely semantic. NCLB and MDE's HQT provisions focus on the *inputs* — such as certification and coursework, which are not associated with student learning gains — rather than the *outcomes* — i.e. student achievement gains — as the measure of teacher quality. To ensure that students are learning in classrooms with highly effective teachers, the state needs to measure teachers' impact on student achievement and design policies to promote the recruitment and retention of effective teachers, while at the same time discouraging and removing ineffective teachers.

Using Value-Added Assessment to Define Teacher Quality

The central premise of "value-added assessment" is that it is possible to measure the contributions that a teacher makes to a student's academic achievement gains. Value-added measurement of teacher quality is not an original idea, even though the statistical tools to perform such calculations have been around for a relatively short time. Many scholars, with varying political perspectives, recognize the benefits of using value-added measures of teacher quality.[123]

---

xxxv   A similar argument is made by The Commission on No Child Left Behind, which advocates for "Highly Qualified Effective Teachers"; however, the commission's arguments about the length of time allowed for teachers to demonstrate that they are effective, i.e., seven years, is questionable. Also questionable is the commission's opinion that peer evaluations should be included in the measure of teacher effectiveness, and that teachers should never have to be assessed for effectiveness again after they meet their proposed HQET standards (see The Commission on No Child Left Behind, "Focus on Teacher Effectiveness to Improve Student Achievement And Enhance Teacher Support: The Commission's Recommendations in Practice," (The Aspen Institute, 2007), http://www.aspeninstitute.org/atf/cf/%7BDEB6F227-659B-4EC8-8F84-8DF23CA704F5%7D/TeacherEffectivenessBriefFINAL6.28.07.pdf (accessed June 26, 2008). The Center for Teaching Quality advocates "Highly Expert Teachers" as opposed to "Highly Qualified Teachers." However, even in advocating the use of value-added measurement, they focus on the limitations of this strategy. "The 'Highly Qualified' Teacher or the Highly Expert Teacher" (Center for Teaching Quality, 2007), http://www.teachingquality.org/nclbhqt/index.htm (accessed May 18, 2008).

Value-added assessment provides us with insights that a simple look at student test scores alone cannot. If, for instance, we were simply to evaluate teachers on the absolute performance levels of students, we would unfairly punish teachers assigned to classrooms with weaker students. For example, using absolute performance levels, we would be forced to say that a teacher with students who score at the 55th percentile on standardized tests is more effective than a teacher with students at the 35th percentile. Through value-added analysis, however, we might show that a teacher who raises average student achievement in her class from the 25th percentile to the 35th percentile is more effective than a teacher whose students perform consistently at the 55th percentile.

The calculations involved in determining the value added by a teacher sift out a variety of factors that contribute to student performance but are unrelated to the teacher's contributions. For example, it is well-established that a student's individual characteristics, such as family income, demographics and English language proficiency, tend to affect his or her success. As described below, value-added statistical models can control for these demographic factors. The models can also control for the influences of a school or of classmates on a student's performance. The goal is to isolate that part of a student's performance gains that result from his or her teacher's skill and effort through the course of a year.[xxxvi]

The National Council on Teacher Quality, a Washington, D.C.-based nonprofit organization that conducts research on teacher quality, lists four ways that using value-added measures can help to promote effective teaching. They note its usefulness in "Identifying professional development needs; Evaluating teachers, provided other criteria are considered as well; Awarding individual bonuses, provided other criteria are considered as well; and Providing the objective data needed for dismissal of an ineffective teacher."[124]

The logical question is, If value-added statistical models are

---

xxxvi Such methods involve statistical regression. For a highly technical discussion of value-added modeling, see Daniel F. McCaffrey et al., "Models for Value-Added Modeling of Teacher Effects," *Journal of Educational and Behavioral Statistics* 29, no. 1 (2004). The index of Gordon, Kane and Staiger, "Identifying Effective Teachers Using Performance on the Job" offers a somewhat less-complicated presentation of the statistics involved.

so helpful, why are they not widely known and used? One answer is capacity. As Daniel McCaffrey et al., statisticians at the RAND Corp., note, value-added modeling "requires extensive computing resources and high-quality longitudinal data that many states and districts currently do not have."[125]

Such concerns have led many organizations — including the NCTQ, mentioned above — to include caveats when advocating the use of value-added measures to evaluate teacher effectiveness. Their hesitation is echoed by numerous key teacher quality scholars who are reluctant to say that teachers should be assessed primarily by how their students perform.[xxxvii] Referencing Daniel Koretz of Harvard University and McCaffrey et al., Harvard University's Murnane and Steele note that value-added methodologies have problems with missing data, teachers with small sample sizes of students, an absence of standardized testing in some grades and subjects, a difficulty in separating teacher effects from classroom or school effects, and most of all, a challenge in estimating "what would have happened to the students' achievement under an alternative scenario."[126] In addition, some researchers (for example, Ballou) raise a legitimate concern about the measurement error, or "statistical noise," that exists with any statistical measurement of student achievement and that becomes worse when more than one exam for a particular student is involved.[127]

It is true that the statistical operations employed to measure teacher contributions to student achievement are not perfect, but it is possible to address many of the concerns about value-added modeling and make useful calculations. Regarding missing data and teachers with small sample sizes, it may be necessary to collect data on some teachers over two or three years to get enough data to make an accurate assessment. The value-added evaluations for new teachers would likewise require

---

xxxvii Concerning objections to measuring teachers by student test scores, Helen Ladd writes: "More generally, why does it make sense to try to hold either teachers or schools accountable for the performance of students? Would it not make more sense to try to make the students themselves more accountable for their performance?" She has a point; holding students more accountable might well make sense, perhaps through exit exams and gateway tests. This topic is not the purpose of a primer on teacher quality. Nevertheless, tracking the success of students is important in holding teachers accountable, too, and it is a useful tool in determining teacher quality. See Helen F. Ladd, *Holding Schools Accountable: Performance-Based Reform in Education*, 11.

waiting for a couple years before making an assessment of the type of teacher a novice will become. (A point of clarification: Value-added assessment typically involves measuring how students improve from the beginning of a single academic year to the end. Including several years of data for a particular teacher does not mean comparing the achievements of one set of a teacher's students to those of the next, but rather combining several years of data on students' single-year improvements under that teacher.)

There are also ways to address the fact that students are not tested in every grade and subject either at the state or local level. Under the state's current testing regime, it would be impossible to evaluate individual teacher contributions in certain grades and subjects, since Michigan only tests students annually in grades three through eight in English and math and less frequently in science and social studies, as Graphic 10 shows.[128]

Graphic 10: Student Testing Currently Required by the Michigan Department of Education

Subject	Grades Tested
English Language Arts	Third through Eighth, 11th
Math	Third through Eighth, 11th
Science	Fifth, Eighth and 11th
Social Studies	Sixth, Ninth and 11th

Source: "MEAP Assessment Administrator Manual," Michigan Department of Education, 2007.

Adding annual testing in grades K-2 and 9-10 and in a wider array of subjects would be useful not only for measuring teacher contributions to student learning, but also as a diagnostic tool for improving student achievement.[xxxviii] The decision to expand the range of grades and subjects tested can be made at the local district level, as the testing requirements imposed by NCLB and the MDE provide a minimum level of testing, not a maximum.

---

xxxviii Ideally, this testing would occur at the beginning and the end of the school year, though testing just once a year is also possible, with the difference between a student's scores between the two years representing the gain (or loss).

And there are basic advantages to requiring testing each year. As Robert Gordon, Thomas J. Kane and Douglas O. Staiger write in a report for the Hamilton Project, a program of the nonprofit Washington, D.C.-based Brookings Institution, one unintended consequence of limiting value-added measurement of teacher performance to only the currently tested subjects could "create unhelpful incentives for low-achieving teachers to leave the tested fields and high-achieving teachers to enter them."[129] Although Gordon, Kane and Staiger think this consequence is unlikely given that currently only a few subjects are tested,[130] this unintended consequence cannot be summarily dismissed. Value-added assessment of teacher performance would raise the stakes considerably for teachers. The perverse incentive for poor teachers to avoid teaching subjects where accountability and performance measurement actually matter for their job security becomes a real possibility. Obviously, this negative outcome is not the only reason to consider adding tests in all grades and subjects, but it is yet another important reason to consider doing so.

Hence, it is valuable to consider ways to extend the use of traditional standardized testing to grades and subjects not currently tested. That said, there are some subjects and teaching settings in which the addition of traditional standardized testing is impracticable. Thus, Gordon, Kane and Staiger are right to suggest that teacher evaluation should be expanded to include a high-quality assessment of any teacher in a grade or subject for which traditional standardized testing may prove unworkable. They recommend the use of "Connecticut's Beginning Educator Support and Training (BEST) program, in which new teachers submit portfolios of their work, including lesson logs, videotaped segments of teaching, examples of student work, and reflective commentaries on the goals during lessons."[131] Perhaps some of the measures included in the BEST system could be helpful — namely principal evaluation — but policymakers should be wary of unintended consequences with these performance measures. It is not particularly clear what can be gained by analyzing lesson logs or reflective commentaries on the goals during lessons.

Researchers do have reasonable concerns about the statistical errors that exist in getting exact point estimates for the value teachers add to student achievement, but the very researchers who point out the flaws in these methodologies have nevertheless continued to use them in their own research. Value-added methodologies are also employed by leading education researchers at Stanford's Hoover Institution, the Brookings Institution, the Harvard Graduate School of Education and the University of Wisconsin. Just as leading education researchers do not let the limitations of these otherwise powerful methodologies invalidate their research claims, reformers who want to employ a more objective measurement of teacher performance as a way to improve student achievement should look to value-added methodologies as a better way of measuring individual teacher quality.

In fairness to researchers who have raised concerns about value-added methodologies in assessing teachers, it is true that value-added models are usually best at detecting the best and the worst teachers, rather than accurately sorting those teachers whose performance lies in the middle range. But given this concern, one reasonable response would be to sort teachers into three broad categories of value-added achievement and compensate them accordingly.

Currently, the Michigan Department of Education does not calculate teacher value-added measures. The MDE is exploring ways to include some version of this concept in determining "adequate yearly progress" under the requirements of the No Child Left Behind Act, but the models that the department is considering would not allow calculations of individual teacher contributions to student learning. At this point, the MDE does not have identifiers in its accountability database that would connect students to their teachers in a given year. Still, the MDE already collects critical individual student information, including student race, gender, poverty status and English language learner status. The MDE also has information about individual teachers and their years of experience and preparation.

Since the MDE does not currently intend to calculate individual teacher value-added, local districts would have to commit data analysis resources to this, or policymakers would need to adopt legislation to direct the MDE to do so. For state officials to undertake this task, teacher and student identifiers would need to be created to allow for the linking of students to their teachers each year. Depending on the exam chosen, yearly scores might have to be adjusted before they could be used in a value-added model. This is largely a mathematical exercise, however, and neither of these steps would be particularly labor- or resource-intensive. In fact, districts and charter schools could expand the use of standardized assessments, just as many conventional districts, charter schools and independent schools already have. For example, the Northwest Evaluation Association reports that more than 100 Michigan districts, charter schools and private schools already contract with the association for test assessments the schools administer in addition to the state-mandated Michigan Educational Assessment Program exams.[132] As of 2008, according to an NWEA spokesman, the association charges approximately $14 per student for these assessment services,[133] so schools interested in regular assessments should find the costs manageable.

Finally, those overseeing a value-added assessment would need to adopt and run the statistical model that would produce estimates of teacher effects. These activities would require expertise and time.

The MDE already has the technical know-how to supervise such a project, though the department might need to hire an additional person to oversee it. Obviously, if value-added assessments were orchestrated through the MDE, the state Legislature would have to pass legislation authorizing the project and its key features.

Alternatively, a school district might implement the project on its own. Individual districts may or may not have the expertise to undertake such statistical modeling, so they might need to hire technically skilled personnel or contract the work to a consulting firm. For medium to large districts, a skilled full-time employee devoted almost exclusively to this project would probably be the more cost-effective option and could likely be hired for around $100,000. Districts can also contract with private research firms that already conduct such assessments. The money to pay for these improvements in teacher and student assessment could be shifted from other less effective teacher quality programs, such as perfunctory professional development activities (see the "Limited Role of Professional Development," Page 112), without increasing total spending.

The larger obstacle to value-added assessments would be collective bargaining agreements. A number of Michigan districts have acquiesced to contract clauses preventing the districts from using student achievement to help determine teacher compensation.

Inevitably, such clauses help ensure that teacher pay is governed by a single salary schedule and that any increase in compensation will occur as an across-the-board pay hike. Since unions almost always prefer these across-the-board hikes, districts without contract clauses prohibiting the use of student achievement in calculating teacher compensation will probably still face union opposition to the implementation of value-added assessment.

Regardless, as noted earlier (see "Across-the-Board Salary Increases," Page 49), across-the-board pay hikes can actually discourage improvements in teacher quality and exacerbate shortages in understaffed subject areas. School boards intent on using value-added assessment to get the best teachers into the classroom may face stiff opposition at the bargaining table, but they will be pursuing a goal that can directly improve how their students learn in the classroom.

Principal Evaluations

Although value-added assessments are defensible for evaluating teacher effectiveness, student test scores need not be the only measure of teacher quality. Principal and vice principal evaluations can also help pinpoint good teaching, and policymakers who face resistance to value-added assessment may want to consider offering to include supervisor evaluations as well. As a practical matter, however, many of the same groups that unremittingly point out flaws of value-added measurements also argue that supervisor evaluations are biased and capricious.

Yet principal or vice principal evaluations are superior to peer evaluations or parent evaluations, which are more likely to suffer from subjectivity.[xxxix] Research findings also suggest that principals are capable of measuring teacher effectiveness.[xl]

---

xxxix For an argument on site-based management reform, see Angus McBeath, "The Edmonton Public Schools Story: Internationally Renowned Superintendent Angus McBeath Chronicles His District's Successes and Failures" (Mackinac Center for Public Policy, 2007), http://www.mackinac.org/archives/2007/s2007-13.pdf10 (accessed May 18, 2008).

xl In a recent report on teacher evaluation systems, Thomas Toch and Robert Rothman of Education Sector, an education policy think tank in Washington, D.C., raise concerns about the current methods of measuring teacher quality (see Thomas Toch and Robert Rothman, "Rush to Judgment: Teacher Evaluation in Public Education" (Education Sector, 2008), http://www.educationsector.org/usr_doc/RushToJudgment_ES_Jan08.pdf

(accessed June 26, 2008)). In particular, Toch and Rothman criticize the common practice of having a single supervisor assess teacher performance through a single classroom observation.

It is valid to criticize the practice of principals' making uninformed personnel evaluations, and it is reasonable to encourage principals to supplement the information gathered through their own observations of teachers with input from lead teachers, parents and students through formal and informal methods as appropriate. However, not all of Toch and Rothman's recommendations for fixing the problems inherent in conventional rating systems are likely to bring about meaningful changes.

Toch and Rothman call for the use of multiple measures and multiple evaluators. Regarding multiple measures, they write: "The experiences of the leading comprehensive evaluation systems suggest that samples of student work, teachers' assignments, and other 'artifacts' of teaching are valuable compliments to classroom observations and should be included in evaluations" (Page 19). Moreover, they write, "To get a fuller and fairer sense of teachers' performance, evaluations should focus on teachers' instruction — the way they plan, teach, test, manage, and motivate" (Page 18). As I argue throughout this primer, teacher performance is best measured by student outcomes. Including these varied measures of teacher inputs sounds compelling, but confuses the central focus of teaching. Planning, teaching, testing, managing and motivating can help a teacher to be successful, but at the end of these efforts, success on these tasks does not guarantee the desired outcome. Thus, teacher evaluation should stay focused on the outcome — student achievement — not the means of achieving that outcome.

Although they do not completely disregard the use of standardized test scores for teacher evaluation, Toch and Rothman argue that "test scores should have a minor role, accounting for under 50 percent of a teacher's evaluation" (Page 18). They refine this recommendation by stating that test scores should not be used to measure individual teacher progress, only schoolwide progress. Toch and Rothman support this claim by writing, "That's because many teachers don't teach tested subjects, the small number of students that many teachers teach skews the results, and using schoolwide scores encourages school staffs to collaborate rather than compete" (Page 18).

The goal of value-added measurement is to improve upon teacher evaluation by centering on the outcomes that matter most. The fact that not all teachers teach currently tested subjects or large classes does not preclude the use of the test scores to measure the performance of teachers for whom we do have sufficient relevant data. Even so, some teachers will need to be measured by schoolwide gains. Under a bonus system, teachers measured by schoolwide gains could have lower potential rewards than teachers who are under higher level of scrutiny. Alternatively, schools can introduce new assessments in a wider variety of subjects. The data from these additional tests could be helpful for diagnosing student progress and for measuring teacher performance. The common complaint that teachers will compete, rather than collaborate, under evaluation systems that use test scores to measure individual teacher performance can also be addressed. Including a schoolwide performance measure for all teachers — including those who will be measured individually — will ensure that teachers continue to collaborate. In fact, it may drive them to collaborate more than before.

A recent RAND Corp. working paper on merit pay by Richard Buddin and colleagues lists some potential limitations to supervisor evaluations of worker effectiveness.[134] The researchers explain that it can be difficult to correct for the inherent subjectivity of any performance evaluation that involves individual supervisor judgment. They add that problems can also arise when workers perceive favoritism and that a subordinate's personality or demographics can interfere with supervisor objectivity. They also note that supervisors may be hesitant to judge performance accurately out of fear of reprisals from disgruntled workers. Finally, they write, "Compression of scores or rankings towards the upper end of the distribution is likely to occur when evaluations are used as part of a pay setting."[135] Buddin et al. also refer to a recent study of principals' ability to evaluate teacher performance by Brian Jacob of the University of Michigan and Lars Lefgren of Brigham Young University.

Jacob and Lefgren asked principals in an unidentified Midwestern school district to rate 202 teachers of core subjects during the 2002-2003 school year in grades two through six on a scale from one to 10 on a number of different traits traditionally seen as related to teacher effectiveness, such as classroom management skills.[136] Jacob and Lefgren also calculated the student achievement test score gains for each teacher. Then they compared principals' ratings of effectiveness to actual effectiveness as measured by student achievement gains. They found that principal ratings and value-added calculations were roughly

---

Concerning the use of multiple evaluators, Toch and Rothman argue that principals often fail to differentiate levels of performance when evaluating teachers. Toch and Rothman suggest that this phenomenon may be due both to the unwillingness of principals and their inability to measure teachers accurately. To address these problems and principals' subjectivity, Toch and Rothman recommend the use of carefully trained peer evaluators (typically senior teachers) whose perspectives can broaden the pool of viewpoints.

Unfortunately, allowing teachers to evaluate one another simply replaces one type of subjectivity with another. Teachers can use evaluations of peers as a way to solve petty grievances and vendettas. The work of the University of Michigan's Brian Jacob and Brigham Young University's Lars Lefgren and of Douglas Harris and Florida State University's Tim Sass indicates that principals are capable of evaluating teachers accurately. The problems with principal evaluations arise under the current system of teacher tenure, in which the process of removing a low-performing teacher is doubtful and can take several years. Principals thus face real disincentives to giving negative performance evaluations and thereby alienating teachers.

equal in identifying the most and least effective teachers, but that principals were less able to differentiate effectiveness in the middle of the teacher quality distribution. They also examined the extent to which a teacher's education and experience, which are the basis of the single salary schedule, are good predictors of student achievement growth. On this question, they found that education and experience were inferior predictive measures of teacher quality.

Interestingly, Jacob and Lefgren found that principal evaluations were better predictors of parent preferences for specific teachers than were the teachers' value-added achievement measures, years of experience, education or compensation. While this finding could be taken as a sign that principals and parents are equally "wrong," the finding probably indicates that principals perceive teacher characteristics that parents tend to value, even though these characteristics may not be measured by standardized tests.

Despite the fact that principal ratings are good indicators of teacher effectiveness in the classroom, Jacob and Lefgren are careful about recommending the use of this rating mechanism. They note that their experiment was carried out in a setting in which principals did not face job pressure to identify effective teachers. They explain that the effect of a higher-stakes environment is unclear: While the increased importance of the evaluation might motivate principals to be even more accurate, it might also make them reluctant to assess teachers honestly for fear of reprisals.[137] (Principals' evaluations were kept confidential and not made available to the teachers themselves.[138])

Jacob and Lefgren also found that principals, regardless of their own sex, routinely discriminated against male and untenured faculty. They wrote: "Specifically, principals rate both male and untenured teachers roughly 0.3 to [0.5] standard deviations lower than their female and tenured colleagues with the same actual proficiency."[139] They offered a lengthy set of possible explanations for this discrimination without any firm conclusion, but stated, "Regardless of the cause, however, this discrimination may place male and untenured teachers at a disadvantage in a system that relies more heavily on principal assessment."[140] Ultimately, this and the study's other findings indicate that although principal evaluations may have drawbacks, they can help identify good teachers.

Recent research findings by Douglas Harris and Florida State University's Tim Sass also suggest that principal evaluations can help identify teacher quality. In a 2007 study, Harris and Sass compared principals' private ratings of teachers in an anonymous Florida school district to value-added calculations of teacher effectiveness.[141] The 30 principals included in the study spanned elementary, middle and high school grades. Harris and Sass wrote, "We find a positive and significant correlation between teacher value-added and principals' subjective ratings and that principals' evaluations are generally, though not always, better predictors of a teacher's value-added than traditional approaches to teacher compensation that focus on experience and formal education."[142] Like Jacob and Lefgren, Harris and Sass advised caution in the use of principal evaluations for use in teacher accountability or reward systems; they do not dismiss this possibility, however.

As this research suggests, principals are generally capable of evaluating teacher effectiveness. Principals' input can be used as a supplement to value-added assessment and to help address concerns over value-added measures of teacher effectiveness.

Part VI: Market-Based Reforms to Improve Teacher Quality

Basing teacher compensation on teacher effectiveness is an essential step in translating better assessment into teacher quality improvements. This chapter discusses how authentic performance pay works, examines differential pay and career ladders (two other reforms that focus on changing teachers' incentives) and explores how lowering barriers to entry into the teaching work force can improve teacher quality.

Merit Pay

When teacher quality is measured by the degree to which teachers affect student learning, as indicated by student test score gains and principal evaluations, other reforms become possible, such as compensation reform. Compensation plans that pay teachers differently for different levels of performance are commonly called "merit pay," "pay-for-performance," or "incentive-based pay" plans. There is no single merit-pay program; rather, the merit-pay programs that have been adopted across the country have various features. For example, some plans reward teachers only for increasing student test scores, while others include supervisor or peer evaluations as measures of teacher merit. Still others include the amount of professional development that teachers undergo as a sign of merit and a basis for pay. Researchers for Vanderbilt University's National Center on Performance Incentives have reviewed various merit-pay plans and provided useful descriptions.[143]

As indicated in Part III, nearly all schools nationwide and in Michigan pay teachers according to the single-salary schedule. Unfortunately, the characteristics on which this pay schedule is based do not correlate with greater student achievement gains. Under the current pay system, teachers are encouraged to help their students learn primarily out of concern for the students and the intrinsic rewards of doing a good job. True, these are significant motives. Teachers tend to enter the profession because of their love of children and their desire to serve others. Still, it is only reasonable to recognize that they, like other people, are motivated to work partly by financial rewards and the recognition those rewards signify.

Without the possibility of earning more money for high-quality performance, teachers may be indirectly encouraged to meet only minimum performance levels, such as maintaining order in the classroom or keeping peace with parents. This outcome is even more likely when teachers are observed only a few times per year by supervisors, and their individual performance is not objectively measured by student test score performance gains. Single-salary-schedule compensation policies have ensured that teachers are paid the same amount whether their students improve or not, and across-the-board pay increases are often guaranteed simply for showing up each year. Unfortunately, as demonstrated in Part I, student achievement in Michigan is not high, and it has not improved compared to the national average despite high and rising state spending. In this context, alternative pay structures make sense. They reward the key people — effective teachers — who can improve public education in the state.

Some U.S. school districts have adopted pay-for-performance for teachers, yet only a few districts in Michigan have even begun to explore the possibility.[144] The current discussion of merit pay is confused by historical debates over pay-for-performance programs. Teacher merit pay has been tried at various times over the past two centuries, and many of these experiments have ended in failure. As Allan Odden and colleagues from the University of Wisconsin found, the chief reason for these failures has been a loss of support from teachers and the public due to difficulties in understanding how pay-outs were calculated, to perceptions that bonuses were skewed by principal favoritism, and to a fear that teachers would be discouraged from collaborating.[145] Still, over the last decade, policymakers in Denver, Florida, Minnesota, Little Rock and elsewhere have attempted to learn from merit pay's past failures and designed plans that appear to be leading to student success.[xli]

In order to evaluate incentive-based programs fairly, merit pay must be distinguished from other reforms, such as differential pay, career ladders and inauthentic performance-pay plans like "knowledge-and-skills-based pay," which provides extra compensation to teachers for participating in extra education and training.[146] As University of

xli For summaries of these plans or synopses and links, see Podgursky and Springer, "Teacher Performance Pay: A Review," or "Reforming Teacher Pay" (Policy Innovation in Education Network, 2007), http://www.edpolicyinnovation.net/pie/template/topic.cfm?topic=24 (accessed May 18, 2008). The plans in these various locations may have some features of "knowledge-and-skills-based pay," but they also have a component that is based on student achievement gains.

Wisconsin researchers Herbert Heneman, Anthony Milanowski and Steven Kimball have written: "A teacher's knowledge and skills are the basic inputs that a teacher brings to the instructional process. These skills include knowledge of content and pedagogy, skill in assessment and classroom management, and general abilities, attitudes, and personality dispositions."[147] Knowledge-and-skills pay plans are often classified as performance pay because they provide financial incentives to teachers not only to improve student achievement, but also to participate in extensive professional development.[148] By contrast, authentic merit pay primarily rewards student outcomes, not teacher inputs. To the extent that such plans focus on professional development, rather than student achievement gains, it is confusing and misleading to classify them as performance pay.

This distinction is important. In public discussion, knowledge-and-skills-based pay, which many teachers unions now claim to support, can easily be mistaken for genuine merit pay. For instance, in September 2007, the U.S. House Education and Labor Committee held hearings on the reauthorization of the No Child Left Behind Act. Reform proposals introduced by committee Chairman George Miller, a Democrat, had included merit-pay legislation that would have based teacher rewards for performance on student achievement test score gains. Education Week's David Hoff reported that Rep. Miller was confused when, at the end of the hearings, "NEA President Reg Weaver and AFT Executive Vice President Antonia Cortese objected to proposed alternative pay programs for teachers, which are included in the section addressing teacher quality."[149] Hoff noted that Rep. Miller reminded the union leaders that the language in the bill had been drafted based on prior conversations with the unions. Yet faced with a true merit-pay program, the AFT's Cortese spoke up and said, "We do have specific concerns about a provision that would use test scores to evaluate teachers."[150]

This exchange in Congress clarifies the characteristics of authentic merit pay. Reconfiguring the teacher salary system to allow principals to award higher salaries or higher raises based on student achievement gains would be a meaningful reform.[xlii]

---

xlii The next section, "Differential Pay," describes how principals could also be given discretion to pay more for teachers in subject areas that are difficult to staff.

Teachers may be uneasy about proposals to alter their base pay, however. Reform-oriented school boards may thus want to propose that teachers get the same base pay, but receive bonuses for their effectiveness in improving student test scores. Most of this section focuses on the use of performance bonuses.

Although recent research (discussed below) demonstrates that merit pay based solely on student achievement gains can improve student test scores, policymakers may want to include the use of supervisor evaluations in merit-pay proposals. Teachers concerned about the use of statistical models to determine their bonuses may be better disposed to a formula that includes a principal's evaluation. A similarly helpful proposal might base merit pay partly on group performance — in other words, rewarding teachers based on how a team of teachers with whom they collaborate succeeds in improving student performance. This approach may be particularly appropriate with elementary and middle school teachers, since they often plan as a team.

How might these recommendations work in practice? One suggestion would be to divide a $10,000 annual maximum merit-pay bonus along these lines: 50 percent would correspond to an individual teacher's students' average achievement gains as determined through a value-added assessment; 30 percent would correspond to the average gains of the teacher's team; and the final 20 percent would correspond to a supervisor evaluation.[xliii] Individual school districts and schools considering merit pay should make their own determinations about the percentages of bonus pay that might used with these three categories.

The exercise should prove worthwhile because merit pay is a viable reform that can indeed lead to greater student achievement. Writing for the National Bureau of Economic Research, David Figlio and Lawrence Kenny used a national sample of longitudinal student data to estimate the impacts of a variety of performance-pay plans related to student achievement. For example, the most restrictive (and hypothetically most motivating) plans were those that "had at least one of the following indicators of high salary incentives: a) at least a 20 percent salary range, b) merit raises that are given to no more than 5 percent of the teachers,

---

xliii For teachers who do not have students whose test scores can be attributed primarily to them, such as resource teachers or music teachers, bonuses would be rewarded for schoolwide gains.

or c) merit bonuses that are received by no more than 7 percent of the teaching staff."[151] Although not all of the student achievement gains associated with performance-pay plans in the study were particularly large (between 1.3 and 3.2 points), Figlio and Kenny found, "[T]he use of teacher salary incentives is associated with higher levels of student performance, all else equal."[152]

Figlio and Kenny carefully noted that not all types of programs have this association, as merit-pay programs "that award bonuses to very large fractions of teachers are apparently not associated with student outcomes."[153] These findings provide strong correlational evidence that teachers tend to act in ways that raise student achievement in schools where meaningful performance incentives exist. This study does have a notable limitation, however, since Figlio and Kenny were able to establish only a correlation between merit pay and student outcomes, not a clear causation.

Many research organizations are now releasing reports with recommendations regarding which features of merit-pay plans will most likely lead to success.[154] Many of these suggestions address not only the key elements of successful reform programs, but also the need to involve teachers in the planning process and to avoid supplanting useful collaboration with counterproductive competition. Reports on merit pay often summarize existing research and make recommendations based on program evaluations of specific merit-pay experiments.

Two such program evaluations are the first- and second-year reports by University of Arkansas researchers of the Achievement Challenge Pilot Project, a merit-pay program in Little Rock.[155] The ACPP bases awards solely on student achievement gains that occur during a single school year. The program has operated for three school years, beginning with one school in 2004-2005, adding a second in 2005-2006 and adding three more in 2006-2007. Thus, by the end of the program, five schools were part of the ACPP.

In January 2007, Marcus Winters, Gary Ritter, Joshua Barnett, Jay Greene and others at the University of Arkansas Department of Education Reform released their first report on the impacts of this program.[156] In this report, they examined the effects of the program in the first two schools and concluded that the students improved by 7 percentile points on average on standardized test scores.

Graphic 11 shows how bonuses were awarded in the Little Rock experiment for four of the schools in school year 2006-2007.[xliv] Teachers earned
rewards based on the magnitude of their students' gains, and other school
personnel — including principals, aides and even custodians — earned
awards based on schoolwide gains. For individual teachers whose students' scores can be directly linked to them (such as a fourth-grade teacher
in a self-contained class), the percent growth was calculated for each student by subtracting the prior year score from the current year score and
then by dividing the difference by the prior year score. These calculations
were completed using normal curve equivalent scores.[xlv] In determining the payout for these teachers, the average percentage of growth for
all students in the class was calculated by adding the individual percentile
growth scores and dividing that sum by the number of students. A teacher
was then awarded the per-child dollar figure for that percentage range
multiplied by the number of students in his or her class.[157] For employees like principals, physical education teachers and music teachers, whose
students' scores could not be directly linked to them, the payout was a
lump sum based on the average schoolwide percentage growth. Individual
awards exceeded $8,000, and personnel in both of the schools included in
the first-year report earned total bonuses of more than $200,000.[158]

---

xliv The table represents payouts in the third year of the experiment; the payouts in the
second year, at the time of the first-year report by Winters et al., were not substantially
different.

xlv In the earlier section "Using Value-Added Assessment to Define Teacher Quality,"
there was a reference to statistical methods that could filter out nonteaching factors that
might lower (or raise) student test scores. These methods involve regression analysis,
and they provide a sophisticated means of determining the impact a teacher has had on
student achievement.

Readers familiar with regression analysis will recognize that this statistical method was
not employed to determine the merit-pay bonuses in the Little Rock experiment (though
regression analysis was indeed used by the University of Arkansas researchers to establish
that the program had a statistically significant effect on test scores). While the Little Rock
model forgoes some of the virtues of statistical regression, it avoids some of its drawbacks,
particularly the problem of making the method of determining the payouts clear and
accessible to everyone affected by the plan, including parents and the public. Nevertheless,
teachers could certainly request the use of statistical regression to determine payouts if
they became concerned that a particular payout program would otherwise fail to account
for, say, their students' socioeconomic disadvantages. In fact, the regression model could
be developed in consultation with them and their representatives, so that they could
assess the potential drawbacks of the model before adopting it.

Graphic 11: The Achievement Challenge Pilot Project Payout Plan for Four Schools in School Year 2006-2007

Employee Type / Position	0-4% Growth	5-9% Growth	10-14% Growth	15%+ Growth	Maximum Payout
Principal	$2,500	$5,000	$7,500	$10,000	$10,000
Teacher[1] (Grades 4 –5)	$50	$100	$200	$400	$11,200
Teacher (Grades 1-3)	$50	$100	$200	$400	$10,000
Teacher (Kindergarten)	$50	$100	$200	$400	$8,000
Coach[2]	$1,250	$2,500	$3,750	$5,000	$5,000
Specialist[3]	$1,000	$2,000	$3,000	$4,000	$4,000
Music Teacher	$1,000	$2,000	$3,000	$4,000	$4,000
Special Education	$1,000	$2,000	$3,000	$4,000	$4,000
Physical Examiner	$500	$1,000	$1,500	$2,000	$2,000
Aide	$250	$500	$750	$1,000	$1,000
Secretary	$125	$250	$375	$500	$500
Custodian (Full-Time)	$125	$250	$375	$500	$500

[1] Teacher payouts are provided on a per-child basis, while all other payouts are for schoolwide performance.
[2] Coaches include literacy, math and instructional coaches.
[3] Specialists includes math and reading specialists, reading recovery specialists, gifted and talented instructors, library specialists, counselors and preschool instructors of 4-year-olds.
Source: University of Arkansas Department of Education Reform. Table reprinted with permission of researchers.

This first research report on the Little Rock program also included survey findings comparing the attitudes of participating teachers with those of teachers in control schools. Participating teachers reported no increase in counterproductive competition among teachers. In fact, these teachers rated the atmosphere of their schools more positively than those in control schools. Moreover, teachers in participating schools reported being less likely to find low-performing students burdensome.[159]

Although the first-year report suggested that a merit-pay program could improve student performance, the analysis did have several limitations, including small sample sizes. The second-year report on the Little Rock program, however, expanded the sample size, provided a stronger control group for comparing teacher attitudes and substantiated the claims of the first-year report.[160] In this report, conducted by a University of Arkansas research team that included Gary Ritter, Nate Jensen, Brent Riffel, Marcus Winters, Joshua Barnett, Jay Greene and Marc Holley (the author), teachers in participating schools were included and compared to teachers in nonparticipating schools across the district. Using appropriate statistical controls in their value-added model, they found that teachers in the merit-pay program were significantly more effective. Survey data from the expanded sample in the second-year report did not show the program having as positive an effect on teacher attitudes as in the first-year report, but the presence of merit pay did not appear to damage the school climate or lead to counterproductive competition.[161]

Concerning merit-pay plans that target individual teachers, Charles Clotfelter and Helen Ladd wrote in 1996: "The limitations of such programs are well known: the lack of consensus about what makes for effective teaching; the fact that gains in student achievement often reflect not just the actions of an individual teacher but also the more general environment for learning in the school; and the growing recognition that rewarding individual teachers encourages them to compete with one another rather than to work cooperatively."[162]

Little Rock ACPP teacher survey data suggests that merit pay for individual teachers does not necessarily degrade the school climate as Clotfelter and Ladd suggest. Moreover, as merit-pay programs have evolved, program developers have more often solicited teacher input and achieved greater "buy-in" from teachers at the outset. Also, the findings of Carolyn Horan and Vicki Lambert, researchers for the Beryl Buck Institute for Education, concerning a related system, the Utah Career Ladder Program, suggested that while some teachers saw increased competition among their peers, not all teachers viewed this change as negative.[163] In addition, merit-pay program developers have learned from past failures and created award systems in which all participants can earn bonuses, rather than just the top few. Perhaps, as a result, recent programs have tended to lead to less divisiveness and competition.

On reflection, this result need not be surprising. While competitiveness under the wrong circumstances could damage team spirit, merit pay does provide incentives that motivate teachers and other building personnel to focus their time and effort on promoting student learning, thus emphasizing the goal that entices many educators to enter the profession in the first place. Moreover, because authentic merit-pay programs reward only teachers who actually produce results, such programs discourage the retention of teachers who are simply in the classroom to draw a paycheck, who cannot communicate effectively or who do not have the problem-solving ability to address students' learning challenges. A system that pressures such teachers to improve or to leave may also help morale, since their presence can depress the spirits of dedicated personnel.

Further, merit pay has the potential to attract a different type of professional to the teaching work force.[164] The current pay structure can have the unintended consequence of attracting risk-averse, lower-performing candidates to the profession. Merit pay, in contrast, promises higher compensation to teachers who may be more tolerant of risk — that is, to those who are willing to make their pay depend in part on their ability to help students learn. It may well benefit morale for teachers to see themselves as part of a more enterprising team.

Some may question whether a compositional change in the teaching work force resulting from the attraction of more risk-tolerant people would be a good thing. Yet risk-tolerance regarding a performance-based salary system is different from risk-tolerance involved in hazardous activities, such as sky diving, for example. Having high-performing, enterprising teachers who are adept at problem-solving and willing to work harder to promote student achievement may be exactly the outcome which policymakers should strive for.

Another potential concern can be raised concerning whether an excellent teacher with students in the top quartile can be compared directly with an excellent teacher with students in the bottom quartile. Might their average gains differ due to the students' dissimilar skill levels and potential for improvement? It is true that there are challenges in identifying exactly what a one-point gain in student performance means at different parts of the performance scale. Nonetheless, there are ways to address this concern. For example, one improvement upon simply using percentile scores to make comparisons of student achievement gains at different performance levels is to use normal curve equivalents. Moreover, when scores are converted to the appropriate standardized scales, comparisons even across grade levels are possible. These conversions are possible using the state achievement tests currently in place in Michigan.

A related challenge involves whether it may be especially difficult to raise the achievement of the highest achievers. It is true, perhaps, that a "ceiling" effect may occur, so that students at the 90th percentile do not have much room to grow. Many high-achieving students may have already maximized their potential, and teachers may find it extremely difficult to raise those students' average performance dramatically. Teachers, however, should be involved in designing performance-pay plans, and they may decide to approach this concern in a number of creative ways. For example, teachers in a given school may decide that teachers of certain classes should have their potential bonus tied more heavily to supervisor evaluations. Alternatively, as noted below, teachers may decide that instructors of advanced students should be rewarded in part simply for maintaining a high level of performance.

Clotfelter and Ladd suggest that ceiling effects (the fact that certain high-performing students have little room to improve) and scaling effects (differential rates of progress depending on whether a student's past performance has been strong or weak) can bias value-added models in favor of low-performing or high-performing students.[165] One way to address these issues is to reward teachers based both on growth and attainment. Practically speaking, this means that program designers may choose to reward teachers of students who have routinely scored above the 80th percentile merely for sustaining or slightly improving the original score.

As with many of the recommendations offered in this primer, adoption and implementation of a compensation system with a merit-pay component could occur either at the local district level or at the state level. Local schools and districts will want to include teachers in the design of a particular plan, however, so local districts, rather than the halls of Lansing, are probably better places to settle the details of how teachers would earn their payouts.[xlvi] There are myriad details involved, after all, and teachers should be involved in making these decisions, since the outcome can affect teachers' willingness to support a merit-pay system.

Fortunately, merit-pay plans have begun to emerge in several locations across the country, so Michigan districts would have a choice of models to adapt to their specific setting. In many of the plans, only a small portion of the merit-pay bonus is based on individual classroom performance (as opposed to professional development or schoolwide achievement), but district leaders drawing on these models can shift the emphasis easily enough. Prominent merit-pay systems include those in Little Rock (see Graphic 11 on Page 83), Houston, Denver and New York City.[xlvii] The latter two programs allow individual schools flexibility in the design of the merit award systems, creating a multiplicity of programs about which it is difficult to generalize.

Part of the reason for the proliferation of teacher merit-pay plans is that the federal government made approximately $100 million available for its "Teacher Incentive Fund" in 2006. The TIF program was designed to promote teacher compensation systems that would use student performance as a part of the basis for teacher pay. This competitive federal grant program has supported a total of 34 performance-pay programs located in over 18 different states and Washington, D.C. Not all recipients of TIF funding were traditional public schools; the New Leaders Inc. charter school network received a grant of more than $20

---

xlvi Many performance-pay programs require a supermajority vote of the school staff for the school to participate. For example, in Chicago's Recognizing Excellence in Academic Leadership program, which uses the Teacher Advancement Program model, participating schools were required to obtain a 75 percent majority vote before adopting merit pay. Including a teacher vote as a prerequisite for program implementation may contribute to the likelihood of a program's adoption and ultimate success. See "Memorandum of Understanding Between the Chicago Board of Education and the Chicago Teachers Union, Local No. 1, AFT, AFL-CIO," http://www.ctunet.com/quest_center/documents/REALAgreement1.3.08.doc (accessed June 25, 2008).
xlvii For information about the Houston Independent School District merit-pay plan, see "Houston Independent School District Project SMART" (Center for Educator Compensation Reform, 2008), http://www.cecr.ed.gov/initiatives/profiles/projectSMART.cfm (accessed May 18, 2008). Regarding the Denver Public Schools Professional Compensation System for Teachers, see "Procomp" (Denver Public Schools, 2008), http://denverprocomp.org/ (accessed May 21, 2008).

million spread over five years for a performance-pay program.[166] No Michigan schools participate in the TIF program, due partly to the fact that of the 143 applications submitted nationwide, only four came from Michigan, a state with 552 conventional school districts and more than 200 charter schools. Yet given the findings presented above, merit pay is an essential teacher quality reform that policymakers in Michigan should consider.

Differential Pay

Confusion over merit pay sometimes occurs when union groups use the term to describe "differential pay," which offers higher compensation to encourage teachers to take jobs in high-needs schools and high-needs subject areas. Differential compensation programs are distinct from merit pay in that differential pay rewards teachers and principals for their decisions to work in settings with chronic vacancies, not for classroom performance per se. Differential compensation can come in the form of higher pay or in the form of loan forgiveness, signing bonuses, housing subsidies or other incentives.

Differential pay is commonplace in other professional settings, including higher education. Liberal arts professors, for example routinely earn less than professors in business departments. Within business departments, economics professors regularly earn less than finance professors.

Two basic economics concepts — substitutes and supply — explain these practices. The concept of substitutes acknowledges that business professors have more higher-paying job opportunities outside of teaching than do liberal arts professors. The concept of supply recognizes that when the labor supply of liberal arts professors exceeds the demand represented by professorships and substitute professions, wages will stay low.

In primary and secondary education, differential compensation means that teachers willing and able to fill vacancies in high-needs subjects or high-needs geographical locations would receive a better compensation package than colleagues of similar seniority, credentials and accomplishment. In Michigan, as in many states nationwide, schools in certain rural and urban areas have difficulty filling positions in special education, math, science and foreign languages.[xlviii] Research also suggests that small rural and urban schools serving disadvantaged students tend to be staffed by less experienced and academically weaker teachers.[167] To address supply-and-demand problems resulting from geography, a compensation system including differential pay components might offer a salary supplement to attract and retain teachers who have either proven their effectiveness or who have the potential to be effective.

It is not uncommon for teachers to gain a few years of experience in a more challenging or remote setting only to leave for easier or less remote settings as soon as the opportunity arises. The American Federation of Teachers agrees that differential pay could help address teacher shortages in hard-to-staff areas and hard-to-staff fields.[168] Researchers who tend to disagree with many of the policies advocated by unions also support differential compensation.[169] For example, the American Enterprise Institute's Fredrick Hess has succinctly written, "Beyond teacher effectiveness, however it is measured, there are several other considerations that districts should acknowledge and compensate: The relative challenges an educator faces, the desirability of the work environment, and the relative scarcity of the teacher's skills." [xlix, 170]

One unresolved question concerning differential compensation is just how large salary incentives need to be to attract teachers into hard-to-staff schools. Researchers for the School Finance Redesign Project at the University of Washington recently released a study that attempted to estimate the appropriate amount teachers should be offered to work in schools serving disadvantaged students.[171] The authors established that a teacher in the private-school labor market is paid more to work in a disadvantaged school, and they suggest that the differential pay in private schools might be a starting point for calculating "combat pay" for

xlviii   In the "NCLB Revised Highly Qualified Teacher State Plan," the Michigan Department of Education states, "There continues to be a statewide shortage of special education teachers as well as a need to improve science (specifically chemistry and physics) and math instruction." The NEA reports these shortages for Michigan in "NEA Student Program."

xlix   As Dan Goldhaber notes, "Private sector compensation, in contrast, generally reflects not only individual attributes (often including an individual's performance on the job) but also the attributes of a particular job." (See Goldhaber, "Teacher Pay Reforms," 7.)

public schools. However, the authors noted serious technical limitations in modeling such wages and were unable to arrive at an estimate.[1] Similar problems face other researchers trying to estimate exactly what should be offered as a bonus or salary supplement. As a practical matter, these problems simply mean that it is currently difficult to predict just what levels of differential pay will be needed; policymakers will have to experiment with various levels and types of differential pay to discover what works.

Nevertheless, education researchers Robert Gordon, Thomas Kane and Douglas Staiger, writing for the Brookings Institution's Hamilton Project, have offered the suggestion that teachers in the top quartile of teacher effectiveness should be offered annual bonuses of at least $15,000 to work in high-poverty schools.[ii] Such an incentive would

---

1   Dan Goldhaber, Kate Destler and Dan Player, "Teacher Labor Markets and the Perils of Using Hedonics to Estimate Compensating Differentials in the Public Sector" (Center on Reinventing Public Education, 2007), http://www.crpe.org/cs/crpe/download/csr_files/wp_sfrp17_goldhaber_aug07.pdf (accessed May 19, 2008). The authors discuss the assumptions of hedonic modeling and its potential limitations in estimating compensating differentials in public school teaching. They note, "[M]odels must completely account for teacher quality[;] otherwise the resulting wage premiums will mask quality differentials." They observe, however, that there are difficulties in measuring teacher quality. They also remark, "[H]edonic wage models implicitly assume that wages are reasonably flexible so that they equilibrate the supply and demand for various teacher and school attributes[,] and this assumption is unlikely to hold, as school districts and schools do not operate within a fully competitive labor market."

li   Gordon, Kane and Staiger, "Identifying Effective Teachers Using Performance on the Job," 19. They also pointed to the recommendations of other researchers about the amounts of differential pay necessary to improve aggregate teacher quality and sorting. They wrote: "There is no settled answer to the question of how large incentives must be to attract and retain high-quality teachers in low-performing schools. Kate Walsh (2005) of the National Council on Teacher Quality suggests that bonuses would need to be 10 to 20 percent of base pay. Others have suggested that even 15 percent is inadequate (Miller 2003), that bonuses would need to be at least $20,000 to have an impact (Rothstein 2004), or that bonuses would need to range between 20 and 50 percent of base salary to attract teachers to the highest-poverty schools (Hanushek, Kain, and Rivkin 2001)." Goldhaber cites another study: "In their 2006 paper, 'Would Higher Salaries Keep Teachers in High-Poverty Schools? Evidence from a Policy Intervention in North Carolina,' Charles Clotfelter ... and his colleagues study the North Carolina Public Schools Bonus Program (for the period from 2001-04), which awarded $1,800 annually to teachers in hard-to-staff subjects and schools. They find that this amount was enough to reduce turnover rates by roughly 12 percent." See Goldhaber, "Teacher Pay Reforms," 17.

require substantial funding increases, which some suggest should be supplied by the federal government.

Ideally, instead of seeking more federal involvement in Michigan's public schools, state and local policymakers might try reconceptualizing how salaries are determined. To increase salaries for certain teachers will require either more discretionary monies for teacher compensation — a tall order in a period of rapidly rising fixed pension and employee health care costs[172] — or a redistribution of existing funds within or across budget items. For example, if a local district were to scrap the single-salary system and pool all the available money for teacher compensation, it could then allocate to each school its appropriate share. Then a principal could pay teachers in different subjects and grade levels the amount necessary to fill his or her staff with the highest-quality personnel he or she could afford.[lii]

Such a scenario would no doubt be a tough sell during collective bargaining negotiations. Still, it would help to address the fact that most schools are currently overpaying some teachers and underpaying others, such as their physics teachers (if they can find some). Although this observation may sound like a value judgment about the inherent worth of physics compared to other subjects, it is not. Rather, it is an assertion that physics teachers are often underpaid because there tends to be a small supply of them relative to the number of teaching positions available and relative to high demand for their skills outside the teaching profession. If teacher compensation were decoupled from the single salary schedule, a principal could likely afford a physics teacher at a genuinely competitive salary and yet still afford a good, but traditionally overpaid teacher in another subject at a more reasonable rate.[liii]

---

lii   By contrast, Goldhaber recommends reforming teacher pay from the state level because "States, unlike localities, have the capacity to develop data and analysis systems that can credibly be used to assess significant areas of shortage, track teacher performance, and/or administer a differentiated pay system. And from a political perspective, it may be necessary to get to the state level in order to buffer some of the negative local political consequences arising from various pay reforms." See Goldhaber, "Teacher Pay Reforms," 25.

liii   For an excellent discussion of the economics of teacher supply, see Loeb and Reininger, "Public Policy and Teacher Labor Markets: What We Know and Why It Matters." A similar point is made by Chester E. Finn, "Too Many Teachers, Too Little Pay," (Hoover Institution, 2005), http://www.hoover.org/publications/digest/2993151. html (accessed May 19, 2008).

Instituting such a system would of course have practical problems, but many of those concerns could be addressed creatively. Though a school district might be wary of challenging all current compensation norms and expectations for existing teachers, it might try bargaining with the unions to allow the hiring of new teachers under a reformed compensation system that would grant principals the discretion to pay differentially.

Fully implementing differential pay across different subject areas or grade levels would probably require abolishing the single salary schedule. Although this suggestion may appear politically infeasible at present, differential pay is quite common in private schools, where teachers with relatively similar experience and credentials often earn quite different salaries. Private-school teachers are sometimes grouped according to experience — zero to five years of experience, six to 10 years of experience, 11 to 15 years of experience etc. — and principals can negotiate salaries with individual teachers based on the school's staffing needs. So, if the annual salaries of teachers in the first band range from $30,000 to $50,000, a principal can offer a new physics teacher $40,000 and a new physical education teacher $30,000. These teachers could receive annual performance raises and still fall within the salary band.

Such an approach may be particularly necessary in urban and rural school districts that have a harder time filling certain positions where the supply of teachers may not be plentiful. Some of these districts already receive supplemental funding based on their count of at-risk students or their geographical isolation,[173] but to the extent this money was found to be inadequate, money for differential pay could be drawn from budgets for professional development (which is generally ineffective; see "Limited Role of Professional Development," Page 112).

Ultimately, the single salary schedule need not be considered sacrosanct, and better options, tailored to address the staffing needs in a local district, can reasonably be brought to the negotiating table. In addition to redistributing money across or within line items at the state and local levels, local districts and schools can also sometimes find support for differential pay incentives from private foundations, which have already demonstrated willingness to support such plans. In Michigan, one creative plan already exists to differentially compensate teachers willing to work in Detroit. The MDE reports:

The Eli Broad Foundation currently has two simultaneous programs operating in Michigan. Part of this program includes the recruitment of high school students from Detroit Public Schools (DPS) to attend Michigan State University (MSU) with full tuition coverage. This program requires a five-year commitment to return to teach, as a Highly Qualified teacher, in DPS. The companion to this program brings "Broad Fellows" (MSU students) into the DPS system over the summer months to assist in providing supplemental instruction to underachieving students. The Broad Foundation has given $6,000,000 to underwrite the cost of these programs in Michigan.[174]

Although there is support for differential pay across the political spectrum, policymakers should know that they will probably not pass such reforms without resistance. Put to the test, unions might choose to stand by the single salary schedule. Moreover, it is one thing for union members to support the idea of paying someone an extra $5,000 to work in an inner-city or remote rural school; it is quite another to institute a policy that would pay a history teacher and a calculus teacher with the same experience within the same building considerably different salaries. Nevertheless, a true differential pay system that can fill vacancies in hard-to-staff positions needs to do just that.

Career Ladders

Michigan policymakers may also want to consider "career ladders," which provide financial incentives for high-performing teachers to continue to work with students in the classroom and help other teachers with instruction. Because teaching has few possibilities for career advancement, highly motivated teachers seeking more responsibility and a better salary may move into administration or leave the profession altogether. Schools do need high-quality personnel in administration, but having good teachers routinely leaving the classroom in search of a greater challenge creates classroom vacancies that may be filled with lower-caliber personnel.

To address this problem, some policymakers have used career ladders, which can allow teachers to take on additional responsibilities, such as mentoring, for higher pay without having to abandon the class-room altogether. Although career ladders are theoretically a promising teacher quality reform, there is not a large body of research on how these programs affect student achievement.

One high-quality study by Thomas Dee of Swarthmore College and Benjamin Keys, a graduate student at the University of Michigan, does evaluate whether career ladders can raise student achievement.[175] Their analysis of the Tennessee Career Ladder Evaluation System occurred long after the termination of the program, but they were able to exploit the fact that the original experiment used a randomized design. Coincidentally, this career ladder system had been instituted at the same time and place as the Tennessee STAR class-size reduction program.

The Tennessee Career Ladder Evaluation System had five "rungs." To advance up the ladder, teachers had to meet certain requirements, but in return, they were offered the chance to earn higher salaries. At the program's inception, participation was voluntary for veteran teachers and required for new teachers, but after the first few years, participation became wholly voluntary. Nonetheless, reports showed that more than 90 percent of teachers chose to participate.

Graphic 12 shows features of the career ladder program, which was in place for 13 years. As the figure shows, all new teachers had to start at Rung 1, but teachers who had already been teaching could be placed at an appropriate career level based on a performance evaluation. The dollar figures are from the 1980s and 1990s, so these rewards were worth more at that time.

Graphic 12: Rungs of the Tennessee Career Ladder Evaluation System

5	**Rung Five: Career Level III** Teachers reaching Rung Five receive a salary supplement of up to $7,000.
4	**Rung Four: Career Level II (five years)** A teacher reaching Rung Four can receive a $2,000 or $4,000 salary supplement for extending his or her work year to 10 months or 11 months, respectively. After five years of Level II certification, a teacher has the option either to renew the certification or request promotion to Rung Five (Level III). Promotion to Rung Five involves a more demanding evaluation.
3	**Rung Three: Career Level I (five years)** Teachers reaching Rung Three receive a $1,000 salary supplement. After teaching with a professional certification for five years, a teacher has the option either to renew the certification or request promotion to Rung Four (Level II). Promotion to Rung Four requires superior performance ratings.
2	**Rung Two: Apprentice Status (three years)** Teachers are subject to review after three years of apprentice status. If they pass that review, they are granted a five-year professional certification, and they move to Rung Three.
1	**Rung One: Probationary Status (one year)** All first-year teachers start here. After being supervised by two tenured teachers for one year and passing a first-year review, a teacher achieves apprentice status and moves to Rung Two.

Source: Diagram assembled from description provided in Benjamin J. Keys and Thomas S. Dee, "Dollars and Sense: What a Tennessee Experiment Tells Us About Merit Pay," Education Next, Winter 2005 .

Performance evaluations at Rungs 1 through 3 were conducted by local district personnel and were usually led by the building principal. For advancement to Rungs 4 and 5, teachers had to pass performance evaluations that were completed by independent evaluators from outside the teacher's district. Dee and Keys report: "The evaluations that occurred at each stage of the career ladder assessed teachers on multiple 'domains of competence' using several distinct data sources (such as student and principal questionnaires, peer evaluations, a teacher's portfolio, and a written test)."[176] Critics of the program asserted that promotion had become routine and not a reflection of merit, since 95 percent of participating teachers were successful at earning Level I (Rung 3) status. However, Dee and Keys point out that advancing to Levels II and III (Rungs 4 and 5) proved to be more difficult, as only 79 percent of teachers passed.

Because the career ladder program coincided with the class-size reduction project, Dee and Keys were able to take advantage of the random assignment of students and teachers to classrooms at the school level. Just as with the analysis of the STAR project, this randomization created relative equality among the classrooms in a given building. Because it is true that there was some diluting of the original randomization over time due to a number of factors, Dee and Keys statistically controlled for any systematic observable differences that may have entered into the sample. Although their adjustments could address any differences in students, Dee and Keys were still faced with a self-selection problem with teachers. In other words, if the career ladder program showed that teachers who participated were more effective at raising student achievement, the researchers could not determine whether their success was due to the program making them more effective or to the fact that those who chose to participate were simply different from — perhaps more motivated than — those who did not. Dee and Keys note, however, that if participating teachers were shown to be more successful, it would not matter whether the program was the cause or simply an indicator. At the very least, the program itself would be a success because it would have identified, promoted and rewarded better teachers.

Dee and Keys determined that participating teachers turned out to be more successful than nonparticipating teachers at raising student achievement. Specifically, they found that students of participating teachers scored approximately 3 percentile points higher in math. These students also scored higher in reading, but the differences were not quite statistically significant. Dee and Keys placed their findings in context when they reported: "The estimated gains associated with assignment to a career-ladder teacher equal 40 to 60 percent of the gains associated with assignment to a class with roughly 15 students rather than 22."[177]

Dee and Keys then disaggregated the results for participating teachers into groups by career ladder level. They found that teachers on lower career ladder levels were responsible for the gains in math and that teachers on the higher career ladder levels were responsible for the gains in reading. Thus, even if participating teachers were more effective than nonparticipating teachers, the findings were not altogether uniform.

Dee and Keys' experiment is one of the few that has measured a career ladder's effect on student achievement, but it is not the only study of career ladder programs. In 1994, Carolyn Horan and Vicki Lambert released an evaluation of the Utah Career Ladder Program, which had been adopted by the Utah Legislature a decade earlier.[178] The enabling legislation for the program allowed school districts to determine which components they would include in their local career ladder program. Some of the possible components were extra compensation for time spent on curriculum development, "inservice training, preparation, and related activities," and "additional pay for additional performance."[179]

Horan and Lambert surveyed principals and teachers to learn about their perceptions of the program and its individual components. The results were mixed. For example, while participants reported that they believed the program was having a positive impact on raising student achievement, they also felt that the performance bonuses were not administered fairly.

Susan Moore Johnson and colleagues at Harvard University summarized a number of qualitative studies of career ladders and also generally report that such programs have mixed results.[180] These collective research findings should indicate that reformers looking to institute a career ladder program need to be sensitive to teachers' needs and preferences, since teachers' buy-in is essential to any reform's success. Policymakers interested in this reform should explore the Teacher Advancement Program models, which include a career ladder component and which currently operate in schools in more than a dozen states nationwide. [181]

In a comparison of 1,200 TAP and non-TAP schools from two states, Matthew Springer, Dale Ballou and Art Peng of Vanderbilt University found mixed results concerning the impact of TAP on student test scores.[182] Springer et al. found that TAP students in elementary grades two through five demonstrated significantly higher gains in math over the course of a given school year. However, the researchers also found that TAP had a negative effect in grades six, seven, nine and 10. Although Springer et al. posited two hypotheses for the apparently disparate impacts of TAP on student achievement in different grades, they are not convinced of these explanations. This study also has limitations. In addition to a small sample size of TAP schools, the study suffers from incomplete data on TAP implementation. Still, because other studies of TAP programs were conducted by researchers affiliated with the programs, this study improves on previous research. Moreover, the authors used a superior, complex statistical procedure to control for the "self-selection" possibility that schools that participated in TAP volunteered to do so because they were already predisposed to pursue higher student achievement gains.[183]

Reforming Certification

As with teacher compensation reforms, lowering barriers to entry into the teacher labor market for intelligent and motivated career-changers and undergraduates considering multiple careers has great potential to impact teacher quality in Michigan. Certification is perhaps the most significant barrier to entry into the teaching profession. As noted in Part III, where certification requirements are described in more detail, the current traditional certification system in Michigan requires that teachers graduate from an approved teacher preparation program and pass at least two licensure tests. The state-approved teacher preparation programs determine the coursework requirements in both content areas and teaching skills. Research on the degree to which teacher certification impacts classroom performance (also presented in Part III) indicates that alternatively certified teachers and even intelligent uncertified teachers perform at least no worse than their traditionally certified counterparts. State policymakers should therefore consider reforms to traditional teacher certification to increase the pool of talented people willing to enter the profession.

The No Child Left Behind Act requires that states certify teachers. NCLB does not, however, specify precisely what teacher certification must require. Thus, even under NCLB, states have discretion about how they will certify teachers.

Four main approaches to teacher certification are conceivable: first, the state could decide to give local districts or schools the discretion to certify teachers at the local level; second, the state could require teacher preparation programs at colleges and universities to change their coursework requirements to make teaching programs more attractive to undergraduate majors in other fields; third, the state could drop the coursework requirements altogether and simply require the passing of a content knowledge or other licensure test; or fourth, the state could make alternative certification programs more attractive and navigable for teachers seeking nontraditional licensure. The first option is ideal because it would give local schools greater autonomy, but the current emphasis on mandatory licensing requirements makes this approach unlikely in the near-term. The second option, though worth exploring, is outside the scope of this book, which emphasizes possible changes within the school system, rather than reforms to university curricula. This leaves the third and fourth options: reforms to teacher testing and alternative certification.

A 2005 annual report on teacher quality from the U.S. Department of Education revealed that in the prior year roughly 35,000 people nationwide received alternative certification, while 170,000 graduated from traditional certification programs.[184] In contrast, Michigan reported zero teachers entering the teaching ranks through alternative methods in 2002 and 2003, with only seven entering in 2004. Over the same three-year period, roughly 1,600 teaching candidates in Alabama, 8,600 teaching candidates in California and 5,000 teaching candidates in Massachusetts received alternative certification.[185] According to the USDOE's 2006 annual teacher quality report, the number of new teachers entering the teaching profession through alternative programs "jumped by more than 15 percent from the previous year, and 47 states now have alternative route programs."[186] The 2006 report showed that in Michigan in the 2003-2004 school year, less than 1 percent of the 8,350 individuals completing teacher preparation programs arrived through alternative routes, versus 22 percent in California, 42 percent in New York and 4 percent in Ohio.[187]

An analysis by Jess Castle and Sandi Jacobs of the National Council on Teacher Quality may indicate why Michigan does not have high-performing career-changers and undergraduates entering teaching through alternative routes.[188] Castle and Jacobs report that Michigan's alternative programs — the "Section 1233b Permit" and "Limited License to Instruct (LLI)" — are not "genuine."[189] The NCTQ argues that genuine alternative certification programs have high admission standards regarding academic ability, but allow reasonably quick certification, without the completion of excessive coursework. In other words, for alternative routes to be worthwhile, there should be a combination of high academic standards for participants, but low requirements for program completion — not the other way around.

Michigan's traditional certification requirements and ineffective alternative certification programs create excessive barriers to entry into the profession. Michigan policymakers at the state level should reform this process by modeling alternative certification routes on the successful programs in other states. Given that NCLB requires that states certify teachers as a part of its "Highly Qualified" teacher provision, it is not realistic to advocate doing away with certification altogether, but certainly Michigan policymakers can make entry into the profession through alternative means a more navigable and attractive process.

Although the teacher labor market is not growing in Michigan as it is in states experiencing major population growth, every year there are numerous teaching vacancies in Michigan's public schools due to retirements and teachers making other career choices. New alternative certification routes would give schools a greater chance of filling these positions, a policy that could help schools in Michigan's large urban centers. State policymakers should study other states that have had success in attracting highly intelligent and motivated new teachers through creative alternative certification programs.

One such alternative certification program is the New York City Teaching Fellows program. Research has shown that this program produces effective teachers (see Part III). To apply for this program, candidates must have earned a bachelor's degree with a grade point average of at least 3.0. Before entering the classroom, the "teaching fellows" must pass the state's basic skills and relevant content-area licensure tests. Participants in this program are then given provisional certificates and participate in intensive preservice teacher training. They also enroll in a master's degree program that will allow them to earn full certification upon completion of three successful years of teaching in the district.[190] The program began in 2000, and it has drawn a large number of applicants since its inception. In its inaugural year, 2,100 applications were submitted for the 325 available slots.[191] For the 2007 program, less than 20 percent of applicants were accepted for the 2,000 slots that are now available annually. Currently, about 8,000 of the city's 78,000 teachers have been a part of the NYCTF program.[192] Fellows earn the same salary as other starting teachers, but they receive a stipend during preservice training and tuition reduction for their master's programs.

Teach for America is another alternative route to the classroom. As noted in Part III, TFA is a private program that works with uncertified academically able recent college graduates. These participants receive some teacher training before being placed as teachers for two years in economically disadvantaged schools. Although there is some conflicting evidence on the effectiveness of TFA teachers, the highest-quality studies suggest that TFA teachers can be more effective than other uncertified and even traditionally certified teachers in raising math achievement, and that they are about the same as other teachers in raising reading achievement.

The TFA program began in 1990 by placing 500 teachers in public schools serving disadvantaged student populations, and Detroit Public Schools began to accept TFA teachers in 2002.[193] Citing the need to lay off a considerable number of teachers at the end of 2004 because of financial problems, DPS discontinued its relationship with TFA. The district had employed as many as 34 TFA teachers.[194]

Currently, there are more than 5,000 TFA members serving in 26 different geographical areas nationwide.[195] Given that TFA teachers tend to be reasonably effective in raising student achievement, it seems unfortunate that the program was ended in Detroit. Michigan districts seeking to fill teaching vacancies should consider establishing a working relationship with the program.

On another tack, state policymakers should review the teacher testing component of certification, since a small reform of teacher licensure testing might improve the existing certification system. As discussed in Part III, teacher testing may be a worthwhile mechanism to establish minimum standards for teacher quality. Despite some research that suggests that teachers who perform better on the current licensure tests tend to have higher-performing students, Michigan policymakers should not rush to impose higher cut points or to make tests harder in an effort to raise teacher quality. In addition to the concerns about unintended consequences raised in Part III, the University of Arkansas' Sandra Stotsky explains that the issues involved in using teacher tests in this way may be complicated. In a recent paper reviewing the research literature about teacher licensure tests and mathematics teachers, Stotsky found that many decisions must be made before licensure tests for mathematics teachers can be designed for the purpose of raising teacher quality. According to Stotsky, these decisions involve determinations regarding "1) the mathematics needed for teaching mathematics at different educational levels, 2) the range of mathematical competence among the students who might be in a typical elementary, middle, or high school classroom, and 3) the demands of the mathematics textbooks and other curriculum materials that teachers may be required to use, especially in the elementary and middle school."[196] Stotsky added, "Some of the details can be informed by research; others require professional judgment."[197]

Thus, the substantive teacher testing reform policymakers should explore is asking applicants to provide their test scores when applying for a teaching position. This data could inform a principal's hiring decisions and help local schools to make decisions about appropriate cut score levels. Policymakers need to address with teacher unions how these scores can be made available to principals. In principle, local schools and districts should be provided the maximum discretion to make hiring decisions.

State policymakers should be wary of calls to adopt licensure tests of applicants' knowledge of pedagogy. A number of other states require such tests,[198] and the National Council on Teacher Quality recommends them.[199] But the NCTQ reports that the Michigan Department of Education doubts the validity of this testing, and the department is right to do so. At present, there does not appear to be any compelling evidence that teachers who pass tests of pedagogy as a part of traditional certification programs are more effective in the classroom. Absent such evidence, there seems little reason to add yet another barrier to entry into the teaching profession.

Other reforms are more promising. The American Board for the Certification of Teacher Excellence, a nonprofit organization based in Washington, D.C., was started in 2001 with a federal grant.[200] ABCTE's primary purpose is to serve as an alternative certification program that uses passage of a teaching skills test and a content knowledge test to help career-changers transition to the classroom. Currently, seven states, not including Michigan, allow ABCTE certification to count as state certification and to qualify teachers as "Highly Qualified" under the No Child Left Behind Act.[201] ABCTE certifies teachers in 11 subject areas, and the process, which must be completed within one year, generally takes six to 10 months.[202] In addition to passing the two tests, participants in the ABCTE program must hold a bachelor's degree from an approved university and pass a background check.

According to a preliminary report on ABCTE conducted by Steven Glazerman and Christina Tuttle of Mathematica Policy Research Inc., participants pay $500 for the program, and they complete a study program to prepare for the two certification exams.[203] From the program's initiation until November 2005, slightly more than 1,000 participants had registered for the ABCTE program, and 109 had successfully completed it. Of that number, 56 had begun teaching full time in American schools.[liv] Most of these were located in Idaho, Pennsylvania and Florida. In a follow-up study, Glazerman and colleagues report that principal surveys of ABCTE teachers yielded generally positive results.[204] With these results in mind, Michigan policymakers should explore a relationship with ABCTE as a way to attract and certify high-quality career-changers into the classroom.

---

liv Steven Glazerman and Christina Tuttle, "An Evaluation of American Board Teacher Certification: Progress and Plans" (Mathematica Policy Research Inc., 2006), http://www .eric.ed.gov/ERICDocs/data/ericdocs2sql/content_storage_01/0000019b/80/28/09/9c. pdf (accessed May 21, 2008). Glazerman and Tuttle report: "The remaining 38 percent of Passport holders are not teaching in a full-time capacity, for a variety of reasons: 10 percent are working in an education-related field but are not in the classroom, and 6 percent are substitute teaching. The majority of the non-teachers indicated some desire to be teaching — 10 percent indicated that they could not find a position; of these, over half specified that it was because the hiring authority would not accept the American Board certification (either the state, locality, or school would not accept it, or they required additional credentials)" (Page 7).

Part VII: Other Practices That Need Reform

Within the public school system, the four reforms addressed above likely have the most potential to improve teacher quality and student learning. Nonetheless, there are a number of other current practices that affect teacher quality and need to be improved.

Discretion in Hiring

Two common practices involving hiring decisions currently interfere with a principal's ability to run a school as effectively as possible. The first is that the power to hire teachers is often not delegated to the principals who run the schools, but rather to superintendents or the district's human resources staff. This can be counterproductive. Principals will usually know the needs of their students far better than district-level personnel will, meaning principals are more likely to hire effective teachers. Furthermore, empowering principals to make key hiring decisions can help strengthen the relationships between new teachers and their principals.

Some who favor a leading role for district officials in hiring teachers argue that district involvement is necessary to maintain equality between a district's schools. They claim that without the district's involvement, some principals will be more successful at competing for personnel, leaving their schools with more good teachers than other schools. Inequalities often occur anyway, however, and they are probably a better reason to remove weak principals than they are to deprive principals of the primary responsibility for hiring their schools' most important personnel. In addition, the value of giving an individual school the greatest level of autonomy to serve its own students should be given real weight. As John Chubb and Terry Moe observed in their landmark book "Politics, Markets, and America's Schools":

> The key to effective education rests with unleashing the productive potential that is already present in the schools and their personnel. It rests with granting them the autonomy to do what they do best. As our study of American high schools documents, the freer schools are from external control — the more autonomous, the less subject to bureaucratic constraint — the more likely they are to have effective organizations.[205]

The second problem related to hiring concerns "seniority-based teacher employment rights." In Michigan, as in many other union states nationwide, collectively bargained contracts often have provisions that grant seniority-determined preferences in layoffs[lv] and in teacher transfers.[lvi] This means that when layoffs occur (usually when schools cut teaching positions due to austerity measures or shrinking enrollments), the district must begin with the employees who have the least seniority. The decision, in other words, is not driven by questions of teacher quality.

Much the same is true of transfers from one school to another: When a teaching vacancy arises in a school building, first preference in filling the position is often given to district teachers with more years of service. When a teacher exercises his or her seniority-based transfer rights, those in charge of hiring may not fill that vacancy with a new teacher or another district teacher with less seniority.

To address these constraints on management's considerations of teacher quality (and student needs), local school boards should negotiate changes to collective bargaining agreements so that principals have the authority to retain teachers based on effectiveness, rather than seniority, when layoffs occur. Especially given value-added assessment data measuring the contributions that teachers make to student achievement gains, principals should be empowered to make decisions about whom to retain.

A second reform to principals' hiring discretion concerns seniority-based teacher transfer rights. One cost of such policies is that principals cannot hire the best candidate to meet the specific needs of a particular student population.[lvii] Some researchers — for example, Susan Moore Johnson of Harvard University and Richard Ingersoll of the University of Pennsylvania — challenge the notion that such union policies harm

---

lv   Technically, the layoffs in question are known as "reductions in force," meaning that employees are temporarily or permanently suspended due to budget cuts or student enrollment declines, not for poor performance.

lvi   An example of the role of seniority in layoff, or RIF, situations can be found at: "Contract Quick Points" (MEA-NEA Local 1, L'Anse Creuse, 2006), http://www .iammea.org/lcea/contract_points.htm#staff%20reduction (accessed May 21, 2008).

lvii   In "Collective Bargaining and the Performance of the Public Schools," Terry Moe writes, "And when contract rules guarantee teachers seniority-based transfer rights, they ensure that teachers cannot be allocated to their most productive uses."

student learning or that such policies, in fact, significantly limit principal discretion at all.[lviii]

But ample research exists to refute this claim. For example, evidence from The New Teacher Project's study of hiring patterns in five large, anonymous urban districts supports the assertion that collectively bargained seniority-based teacher employment rights have impaired principals' hiring discretion. Jessica Levin, Jennifer Mulhern and Joan Schunck, the study's authors, found that in a given year approximately 40 percent of vacancies were filled by teachers exercising their seniority-based employment rights.[206] Although the veteran teachers who filled those slots might have been the principals' first choices anyway, the study suggests the vacancies were not filled by the best available candidates.

In a recent study from the Thomas B. Fordham Institute, Frederick Hess and Coby Loup review the collective bargaining agreement in Detroit and report that principals may well be restricted in hiring decisions because of seniority-based transfer preferences.[207] In an earlier Fordham Foundation study, Steven Adamowski, Susan Bowles Therriault and Anthony Cavanna surveyed school principals from a cross section of schools. These principals worked in district schools in three states, and through surveys and interviews, the researchers sought "to determine principals' perceptions of their ability to influence the various functions of their schools; those functions that principals perceive as most important in meeting school performance goals and

---

lviii In "Who Stays in Teaching and Why: A Review of the Literature on Teacher Retention," Susan Moore Johnson, Jill Harrison Berg and Morgaen L. Donaldson supported their argument by citing Richard M. Ingersoll, "Out-of-Field Teaching, Educational Inequality, and the Organization of Schools: An Exploratory Analysis" (Center for the Study of Teaching and Policy, 2002), http://depts.washington.edu/ctpmail/PDFs/OutOfField-RI-01-2002.pdf (accessed May 21, 2008). Johnson, Berg and Donaldson wrote: "Many people believe that principals' hands are tied by bureaucratic and union restrictions when they assign teachers. However, Ingersoll concludes: '[S]chools with unions do not have more out-of-field teaching' (p. 25). His analysis shows that, even with the many constraints on their discretion — teacher union work rules, seniority-based assignments, school district regulations, class-size guidelines, and contractual regulations — principals still have 'an unusual degree of discretion in staffing decisions.'"
Conversations with members of Michigan's education community suggest that there is variation in the discretion in hiring that principals have in districts across Michigan. In some districts, the superintendent's office is primarily responsible for these decisions, while in others, principals play an integral role.

accountability demands; and those areas where principals' lack of control constituted a serious barrier to effective leadership in raising student achievement."[208] One hundred percent of principals in this study reported perceiving control over hiring to be essential, but only 26.7 percent felt that they had a "great deal of autonomy" in this area.[209]

Thus, research supports the contention that principals face restrictions on local hiring due to seniority-based teacher employment rights, but this evidence does not consider the negative unintended consequences that result from such policies. One such consequence of seniority-based transfer policies is that schools serving disadvantaged students often find themselves staffed with lower-quality teachers.[210] When district contracts give teachers with seniority the option to choose their school of assignment, teachers routinely choose to move out of schools serving disadvantaged students.[211] As Marguerite Roza and Paul Hill wrote in a paper published by the Brookings Institution on intradistrict spending inequities:

> Teachers leave these assignments in part because they are not
> compensated differentially at a high enough level to encourage
> them to stay. These teachers value the perceived benefits of
> working in a school with fewer disadvantaged students, such as
> fewer discipline problems and students who are more ready to
> learn, over any monetary benefit they receive in schools with more
> disadvantaged students.[212]

This teacher sorting impacts the teacher quality distribution because high-poverty schools must constantly fill vacancies with beginning teachers, and research shows that beginning teachers are generally less able, at least in their first few years. By comparison, schools in wealthier areas benefit from having a much larger applicant pool from which to choose, thereby increasing the probability that they will select the most effective teachers to meet their particular students' needs.[213]

Reforming Teacher Tenure Practices

Teacher tenure policies make it extremely difficult for a principal to discontinue the employment of tenured teachers. These policies were originally instituted as a way to protect teachers from arbitrary treatment by principals. In Michigan, teachers become eligible for tenure after four years of satisfactory teaching.[214] Ideally, because the current policy protects ineffective veteran teachers at the expense of their students, local schools would do away with tenure and contract with individual teachers on a yearly at-will basis, as is commonplace among private schools. In public schools, at-will teacher employment does exist, particularly in Southern states where unions are less powerful. In Michigan, at-will employment also exists among charter schools,[215] but the unions have successfully prevented it from coming to the conventional school districts. At this point, eliminating teacher tenure altogether would be an extremely contentious process, but Michigan policymakers may want to consider two other reforms.

First, policymakers should consider lengthening the probationary period before teachers can be given tenure.[lix] As noted above, under the current system, teachers are eligible for tenure after four years.[216] Satisfactory service is measured by two annual supervisor observations, which inform a yearly evaluation.[lx] As discussed earlier in the book, education research suggests that if a teacher has not proven himself or herself by the fifth year, he or she probably never will. Nonetheless, the reason I recommend lengthening the probationary period is to give principals greater ease in removing unsatisfactory personnel. Even when it is procedurally possible, sometimes the culture of schools can make it politically costly for principals to remove borderline personnel quickly.

---

lix   The National Council on Teacher Quality recommends that states not guarantee tenure until after five years. It also states, "Apart from observations, teacher evaluations should consider objective evidence of student learning, including the value a teacher adds not only as measured by standardized test scores, but also by other classroom-artifacts, such as tests, quizzes, and student work."
The inclusion of "other classroom-artifacts" with standardized student test scores may dilute the focus on teacher quality. If such class work contributes to the learning that matters, the standardized tests will capture it. Policymakers should be careful not to create policies that punish teachers who do not follow the latest teaching trends, particularly when their students are performing at a high level on standardized tests.
lx   Michigan Federation of Teachers writes: "The purpose of tenure is to provide a measure of job security for teachers, protection against arbitrary employment practices and political or personal patronage, and protection for academic freedom, fostering a classroom environment conducive to learning and open inquiry." Notably missing from this description is a comment about promoting student learning. "What Every Member Should Know About Your Tenure Act Rights" (Michigan Federation of Teachers and School Related Personnel, 2005), http://aftmichigan.org/members/handbook/tenure.html (accessed May 21, 2008).

Second, the criteria used in performance evaluations that are part of tenure decisions should include value-added measurement. As indicated above, principal observations are a useful mechanism for measuring teacher quality, but principals should also use objective value-added assessment measures of student achievement on standardized tests to inform tenure decisions. Of course, local school boards may need to negotiate changes to local collective bargaining agreements to allow student achievement to be included in evaluations on which tenure is based.[lxi]

Improving Teacher Preparation Programs

As with other factors that affect teacher quality, considerable attention has recently been given to the role of traditional teacher preparation programs in improving the teacher work force. This book has touched on this subject only briefly partly because such a line of inquiry demands considerable independent treatment and partly because it lies outside the realm controlled by policymakers within the primary and secondary public school system. Nevertheless, meaningful improvements to teacher preparation might result from rating teacher preparation programs based on the performance of their graduates as teachers in the classroom. If the state kept a database of student performance gains of individual teachers, researchers could determine the general effectiveness of teachers who graduate from the state's various teacher preparation programs. Publicizing such findings would enable teaching candidates to make informed decisions about the programs they choose and help principals make better-informed decisions about which graduates to hire. Finally, such ratings would also encourage less effective programs to improve by modifying their existing practices.[217]

Limited Role of Professional Development

Research organizations and teachers unions often recommend that more money and time be set aside for teachers' professional development activities.[218] As a matter of state law, Michigan requires new teachers to complete 15 days of professional development over their first three

---

lxi The Teachers' Tenure Act does not appear to prohibit the use of value-added assessments in determining whether a teacher is performing satisfactorily for the purposes of obtaining tenure. (See MCL 38.71; MSA 15.1971, §3a(1).)

years.[219] In addition, new teachers, like experienced teachers, must complete five days of professional learning annually.[lxii]

Most research on professional development simply reports the types of training that teachers have said are helpful. Such research tends to analyze teachers' self-reported survey responses about various professional development activities.[220] Although these studies may provide some guidance about professional development design, they are less compelling because they do not provide empirical evidence of student achievement gains. Regarding professional development, the conclusions of Susanna Loeb and Michelle Reininger suggest the need for caution: "Some high-quality professional development programs have been shown to improve teacher effectiveness; however, we do not know whether investment in these programs is more beneficial than equal investment in other school resources, nor what aspects of these programs are particularly beneficial in a given context."[221]

I am unaware of any high-quality studies using value-added calculations that link participation in any professional development programs to greater effectiveness in the classroom in American schools. It seems reasonable to think that teachers could benefit from learning how to use new instructional technology or strategies for classroom management, but it is equally reasonable to question whether so much time and money should be invested in professional development generally. Moreover, the quality of most professional development is suspect. As the University of Michigan's Heather Hill recently wrote: "Although short workshops might be effective in providing piecemeal instructional activities or very general ideas, many scholars believe that given the complexity of teachers' work, short workshops have little effect on teaching or learning."[222]

---

lxii   The Michigan Department of Education states: "There are four sections in the Michigan School Code that address professional learning. Sections 1526 and 1527 specify requirements for the professional learning of teachers. Section 1246 specifies continuing education requirements for school administrators. Section 101(11) enables schools to schedule up to 38 hours of professional learning and count it as part of the required 1,098 hours of instructional time." "Questions and Answers About Professional Learning, New Teacher Induction and Mentoring, and Continuing Education Requirements for School Administrators" (Michigan Department of Education, 2006), http://michigan.gov/documents/Q&A_Revised_Sept_2004_A_100964_7.doc (accessed May 21, 2008).

Until research can demonstrate that teachers who participate in certain professional development definitively raise student achievement, the state should consider paring down current professional development requirements and monies in favor of programs with a better record of success.

Conclusion

Michigan's student achievement trends suggest that something needs to change in the state's public education system. Spending on the state's primary and secondary schools has increased considerably, while student achievement in Michigan is stagnating and even losing ground compared to national averages.

The consensus in education research is that among the factors that schools can control, teachers matter most. It is time for the state to consider reforms that focus on teacher quality.

The first step in improving teacher quality is redefining what is meant by a "highly qualified" teacher. The phrase should mean more than the teacher's possessing state certification and passing marks on a few basic tests; rather, it should indicate that a teacher is highly effective at improving student achievement. These are the teachers Michigan needs.

Teachers' effectiveness can be measured using "value-added assessments," which measure the learning gains that a teacher's students demonstrate during the school year on standardized tests. Reconceptualizing teacher quality in this way opens the door to important market-based reforms that can help improve student learning.

Within Michigan's public school system, the reform with perhaps the most potential to attract and retain effective teachers is performance pay, which rewards teachers primarily for gains in student achievement as measured on standardized tests. This merit-based pay structure can motivate existing teachers and attract high-quality undergraduates and career-changers to the field. Concerns over the fairness of value-added measurements can and should be addressed by conferring with the teachers themselves. Including principal evaluations and rewards for belonging to effective teams of teachers may also help pinpoint quality teaching and ensure effective teachers are not inadvertently overlooked in a merit-pay system.

Another reform that could improve teacher quality is differential pay, which departs from the standard practice of compensating teachers based solely on their years of experience and academic credentials. Under a system of differential pay, higher salaries are paid to teachers in high-demand fields like math and science and in underserved urban and rural areas with disadvantaged students.

Additionally, policymakers should consider evaluating teachers annually based on principal observations and student achievement gains, while loosening restrictions on terminating teachers who show they are not improving student learning. To encourage better teachers to enter the field, policymakers should also lower barriers to entry for career-changers and for academically talented undergraduates through the implementation of reasonable alternative certification programs.

Such reforms will work best in tandem. No single reform is a silver bullet, although some, such as merit pay, could produce noticeable improvements on their own.

To provide context for the discussion of teacher-quality reforms, this book has reviewed the effectiveness of across-the-board salary increases and class-size reductions in improving teacher quality. These reforms appear to be at best inefficient solutions for Michigan's public education problems.

In addition to these primary recommendations, policymakers should also address other practices that affect teacher quality. In particular, state and local policy should allow principals greater discretion in hiring, tie tenure evaluations to a teacher's demonstrated ability to improve student achievement and consider reducing the role of professional development, which has not been shown to lead to better student outcomes. Teacher preparation programs and requirements should also be reviewed to ensure they do not provide unnecessary barriers to entry into the teaching profession; it is unclear that many of the requirements of these programs actually promote effective teaching.

This primer focuses on teachers because they are the key to student learning. A fundamental change in the incentives teachers face will encourage and reward them for doing what most entered the field to do anyway: help children learn. Education policymakers can no longer afford to ignore the reality that teachers respond to incentives — both intended and unintended — and that policies that protect low-performing teachers at the expense of student achievement must be replaced.

Appendix:
The Constitutionality
of Teacher Merit
Pay in Michigan

By Patrick J. Wright[lxiii]

Michigan's most recent state constitution became effective in 1963, and one of its sections could be incorrectly used by opponents of merit pay to argue that merit pay is unconstitutional. Const 1963, art 11, § 6 states:

> By ordinance or resolution of its governing body which shall not take effect until approved by a majority of the electors voting thereon, unless otherwise provided by charter, each county, township, city, village, school district and other governmental unit or authority may establish, modify or discontinue a merit system for its employees other than teachers under contract or tenure. The state civil service commission may on request furnish technical services to any such unit on a reimbursable basis.

Specifically, a question arises about the statement that a local government entity "may establish, modify or discontinue a merit system for its employees other than teachers under contract or tenure." Public school teachers would seem necessarily to be under contract or tenure, and some could argue the provision suggests that teachers cannot belong to a merit-pay system.

xiii Patrick J. Wright, the Mackinac Center for Public Policy's senior legal analyst, is a former Michigan Supreme Court commissioner and assistant state attorney general.

But thorough analysis shows this reading to be incorrect. The constitutional delegates merely sought to exempt teachers from a process that local governments could use to create "a merit system" — a term of art that the constitutional delegates used to denote a kind of civil service system. The delegates did not mean to prevent teachers from receiving merit pay.

When interpreting the constitution, Michigan courts look to the common understanding of the disputed provision. *Lapeer Co Clerk v Lapeer Circuit Court*, 469 Mich 146, 155 (2003). "Words must be given their ordinary meanings, and constitutional convention debates and the Address to the People, 2 Official Record, Constitutional Convention 1961, p 3355, are relevant, although not controlling." *Id.* at 156. In *Studier v Michigan Public School Employees' Board*, 472 Mich 642 (2005), the Michigan Supreme Court stated, "the proper objective in consulting constitutional convention debates is not to discern the intent of the framers in proposing or supporting a specific provision, but to determine the intent of the ratifiers in adopting the provision." *Id.* at 656. The court explained:

> The debates must be placed in perspective. They are individual expressions of concepts as the speakers perceive them (or make an effort to explain them). Although they are sometimes illuminating, affording a sense of direction, they are not decisive as to the intent of the general convention (or of the people) in adopting the measures.

> Therefore, we will turn to the committee debates only in the absence of guidance in the constitutional language ... or when we find in the debates a recurring thread of explanation binding together the whole of a constitutional concept.

Id.

What eventually became Article 11, § 6 began as Committee Proposal 76 at the 1961 Constitutional Convention.[lxiv] Many local units of government had been frustrated by Legislative inaction or Legislative hostility to the creation of local civil service plans. 1 Official Record,

---

lxiv The debates are titled "State of Michigan Constitutional Convention 1961 Official Record," despite the fact that the convention extended from 1961 into 1962.

Constitutional Convention of 1961 at 1752. The crux of that Committee Proposal 76 was to create a legislative bypass that would allow Michigan's localities — more than 1,500 at the time — to individually determine if they wanted to create a civil service system. 1743-44.

Because the original proposal was unclear about which local units of government would be permitted to create a merit system, those units, including school districts, were spelled out in an amendment that was later adopted. *Id.* at 1749, 1765. That same amendment required that a majority of the voting electors of that unit of government approve the process at an election. *Id.*

Some delegates expressed concern about the inclusion of school districts, given that many teachers were covered by the Teachers' Tenure Act and therefore did not need civil service laws. *Id.* at 1754. Other delegates responded that school districts should be included anyway because the districts employed more than just teachers. *Id.* at 1754-56.

The Teachers' Tenure Act was enacted in 1937. 1937 PA 4. Then, as now, the law basically gave tenure to teachers who completed a probationary period, which is currently four years. The law made rehiring the most senior teacher with appropriate credentials a priority following any layoff.

During the constitutional convention, the Teachers' Tenure Act applied only to districts wherein the electors had voted to implement the act. It was not until 1964 that the law was universally applied in Michigan. See 1937 PA 4 at art. VIII, § 1; 1964 PA 2, § 1.

Thus, during the constitutional convention, delegates raised questions about how any new civil service plans created by a school district would apply to districts whose teachers were governed by the tenure act as well. 1 Official Record, Constitutional Convention of 1961 at 1756-57.

The debates show that the concept of "merit system" was not meant to be synonymous with pay for performance, or "merit pay." Overwhelmingly, delegates were using "merit system" as a synonym for "civil service." A couple of other delegates thought the phrase might be confusing in the school context, however. For example, Delegate Faxon stated:

I am looking at the words "merit system" and the words "merit system" may have a definite meaning when you talk with regard to civil employees of cities, townships, counties and villages. But it has a different connotation when you discuss it in terms of schools and teachers. Now, if the intent of this is not to include teachers, then you would have to put in nonteaching personnel in school districts and I would have no objection to such an addition.

Id. at 1757. Later, Delegate Faxon continued:

My only worry is not in the teachers as far as the security of their job is concerned, but in the introduction of another idea which is that of a merit pay system. Now, I don't want to get into the whole merits of this, but it just seems to me that the use of the words here tends to give the impression that this is something that could be done just as one would adopt teacher tenure, or something of that sort. I, for one, choose not to get involved in that particular conflict.

Id. at 1758. In other words, Delegate Faxon was concerned that the constitutional provision as it stood at the time would imply to local voters that they could establish a merit-pay system for teachers by a popular vote.

The next speaker, Delegate Hanna, was the author of the disputed amendment that had included school districts. He indicated that "merit system" and "merit pay" meant different things:

Mr. Faxon, if I thought that I could slip into this constitution a provision for merit pay for teachers, I certainly would do it; but I am sure that a merit system merely means a classification based upon the job held and the length of time in grade and the qualification for that grade. And we have never applied the bonus or piecework system to the janitor or to the top executive in any civil service. I think your worries that "merit system" may go to the argument in the school system concerning merit pay are unreasonable.

Id. A request to strip school districts from the proposal failed. *Id.*

An amendment proposed later sought to change the words "merit system" to "civil service system." *Id.* at 1762-63. This request was made by two delegates who were concerned about potential confusion over the phrase "merit system" in relation to school districts. *Id.* at 1763.

Delegate Hanna then recommended a way to obviate the concern: "May I suggest that you withdraw your amendment and after the word 'employees' put 'except teachers under contract or tenure' so that it is clear that the civil service within school districts does not extend to teachers under contract or tenure." *Id.* Note that there was no indication that this compromise language was meant to foreclose merit pay in the schools. That language was offered to remove any confusion between a "merit system" and "merit pay" for teachers whenever a school district considered the implementation of a civil service system. (Note that the language also removed any conflict between a district's civil service system and the Teachers' Tenure Act by exempting teachers covered under the act from a civil service system.) One of the delegates concerned about the impact of the provision on the schools stated, "It seems clear that the intent of the amendment was not to encompass school teachers and the additional words here would take this into account." *Id.* This amendment was approved and made part of the proposal. *Id* at 1764.

The Address to the People after the convention set out the language of article 11, § 6, and then stated:

This is a new section permitting the establishment, modification or discontinuance of civil service merit systems in political subdivisions of the state, providing a majority of the voters of the unit affected approve. Teachers under contract or tenure are excluded in the provision. The state civil service commission is authorized to furnish technical services to local units on a reimbursable basis, if requested.

2 Official Record, Constitutional Convention of 1961 at 3405-06.

Thus, article 11, § 6, was enacted to create a shortcut, allowing localities to enact a civil service plan without any action on the part of the Michigan Legislature. Teachers were exempted from this shortcut because the delegates believed that the Teachers' Tenure Act acted sufficiently like "a merit system" (i.e. like a civil service system), and the delegates wanted that act to take precedence. The fact that teachers were exempted from this civil service shortcut in no way indicated that the Legislature or local school districts were precluded from allowing pay for performance (that is, merit pay).

Since 1963, the Michigan Legislature has not behaved as if merit pay were impermissible. Michigan Public Act 289 of 1995 contains a provision that states, "A school district or intermediate school district may implement and maintain a method of compensation for its employees that is based on job performance and job accomplishments."[223]

ABOUT THE AUTHOR

Marc J. Holley, an adjunct fellow with the Mackinac Center for Public Policy, is a doctoral academy fellow in public policy at the University of Arkansas. His experience in education includes six years as a private school administrator and teacher and two years as an education policy analyst at the Office for Education Policy at the University of Arkansas Department of Education Reform. He has conducted program evaluations of merit-pay and educational-technology interventions, and he has published numerous editorials, book reviews and scholarly articles for education policy think tanks and in peer-reviewed journals. Before his career in education, Holley served as a nonprofit management consultant in the Peace Corps in Romania. Holley earned a bachelor's degree in classics, cum laude, from Harvard University and a master's degree in education administration and policy from the University of Georgia.

Endnotes

1   "The Nation's Report Card: Overview" (National Center for Education Statistics, U.S. Department of Education, 2008), http://nces.ed.gov/nationsreportcard/about (accessed July 9, 2008).

2   "State Profiles: The Nation's Report Card" (National Center for Education Statistics, U.S. Department of Education, 2008), Michigan profile, http://nces .ed.gov/nationsreportcard/states/ (accessed June 13, 2008).

3   Ibid.

4   "Core of Common Data" (National Center for Education Statistics, U.S. Department of Education, 2008), http://nces.ed.gov/ccd/ (accessed May 8, 2008).

5   Ibid., and "Overview of BLS Statistics on Inflation and Consumer Spending" (U.S. Bureau of Labor Statistics, 2008), CPI Inflation Calculator, http://www.bls .gov/bls/inflation.htm (accessed June 11, 2008).

6   Ryan S. Olson, "Michigan Rankings on National Education Test Fall in 8th Grade, Stagnate in 4th; Proficiency Scores Flat" (Mackinac Center for Public Policy, 2007), http://www.mackinac.org/9010 (accessed May 8, 2008).

7   "May 2007 State Occupational Employment and Wage Estimates" (U.S. Bureau of Labor Statistics, 2008) http://www.bls.gov/oes/current/oes_mi.htm#b15-0000 (accessed June 15, 2008). This ranking is of state mean salaries for elementary school teachers, except special education.

8   "Public Education Finances 2006" (U.S. Census Bureau, 2008), http://ftp2.census .gov/govs/school/06f33pub.pdf (accessed June 13, 2008); "Statistical Tables: Public Elementary-Secondary Education Finances: 2004-05" (U.S. Census Bureau, 2008), http://ftp2.census.gov/govs/school/elsec05_sttables.xls (accessed May 8, 2008).

9   "IES National Center for Education Statistics Common Core of Data Build a Table: 2004-2005 Data, Per Pupil Ratios [State], Total Current Expenditures for Public El-Sec Per Student (State-Fin.)" (National Center for Education Statistics, 2008), http://nces.ed.gov/ccd/ (accessed June 13, 2008).

10 Dan D. Goldhaber, "The Mystery of Good Teaching: Surveying the Evidence on Student Achievement and Teachers' Characteristics," *Education Next* 2, no. 1 (2002).

11 Eric Hanushek and Steven G. Rivkin, "How to Improve the Supply of High Quality Teachers," *Brookings Papers on Education Policy 2004*, ed. Diane Ravitch (Brookings Institution, 2004).

12 Ibid. See similar findings in William L. Sanders and June Rivers, "Research Progress Report: Cumulative and Residual Effects of Teachers on Future Student Academic Achievement: Tennessee Value-Added Assessment System" (University of Tennessee Value-Added Research and Assessment Center, 1996), http://www.cgp.upenn.edu/pdf/Sanders_Rivers-TVASS_teacher%20effects.pdf (accessed May 8, 2008).

13 Linda Darling-Hammond, "Teacher Quality and Student Achievement: A Review of State Policy Evidence" (Education Policy Analysis Archives, 2000), http://epaa.asu.edu/epaa/v8n1/ (accessed June 25, 2008).

14 Terry M. Moe, "Collective Bargaining and the Performance of the Public Schools"

(Education Working Paper Archive, 2007), http://www.uark.edu/ua/der/EWPA/Research/Achievement/1795.html (accessed May 8, 2008).

15 Goldhaber, "The Mystery of Good Teaching: Surveying the Evidence on Student Achievement and Teachers' Characteristics"; Steven G. Rivkin, Eric Hanushek and John F. Kain, "Teachers, Schools, and Academic Achievement," *Econometrica* 73, no. 2 (2005).

16 Dale Ballou and Michael Podgursky, "Reforming Teacher Preparation and Licensing: What Is the Evidence?," *Teachers College Record* 102, no. 1 (2000).

17 Richard J. Murnane and Jennifer L. Steele, "What Is the Problem? The Challenge of Providing Effective Teachers for All Children," *The Future of Children* 17, no. 1 (2007). The evidence they cite comes from Eric Hanushek, "Teacher Characteristics and Gains in Student Achievement: Estimation Using Micro Data," *The American Economic Review* 61, no. 2 (1971); Ronald Ferguson and Helen F. Ladd, "How and Why Money Matters: An Analysis of Alabama Schools," *Holding Schools Accountable: Performance-Based Reform in Education*, ed. Helen F. Ladd (Washington, D.C.: Brookings Institution Press, 1996); R. G. Ehrenberg and D. J. Brewer, "Do School and Teacher Characteristics Matter? Evidence from High School and Beyond," *Economics of Education Review* 13, no. 1 (1994). This point is also made by Sandra Stotsky and Lisa Haverty, "Can a State Department of Education Increase Teacher Quality? Lessons Learned in Massachusetts," *Brookings Papers on Education Policy 2004*, ed. Diane Ravitch (Brookings Institution Press, 2004).

18 Robin Henke, Xianglei Chen and Sonya Geis, "Progress through the Teacher Pipeline: 1992—93 College Graduates and Elementary/Secondary School Teaching as of 1997" (National Center for Education Statistics, U.S. Department of Education, 2000), http://nces.ed.gov/pubs2000/2000152.pdf (accessed May 8, 2008).

19 Susanna Loeb and Michelle Reininger, "Public Policy and Teacher Labor Markets: What We Know and Why It Matters" (Education Policy Center, Michigan State University, 2004), http://www.epc.msu.edu/publications/publications.htm (accessed May 8, 2008).

20 Eric Hanushek and Richard Pace, "Who Chooses to Teach (and Why)?" *Economics of Education Review* 14, no. 2 (1995).

21 E. Vegas, R.J. Murnane, and J.B. Willet, "From High School to Teaching: Many Steps, Who Makes It?" *Teachers College Record* 103, no. 3 (2001).

22 Loeb and Reininger, "Public Policy and Teacher Labor Markets: What We Know and Why It Matters."

23 Henke, Chen and Geis, "Progress through the Teacher Pipeline: 1992-93 College Graduates and Elementary/Secondary School Teaching as of 1997."

24 Sean P. Corcoran, William N. Evans and Robert M. Schwab, "Women, the Labor Market, and the Declining Relative Quality of Teachers," *Journal of Public Policy Analysis and Management* 23, no. 3 (2004).

25 Ibid., 466.

26 Caroline Hoxby and Andrew Leigh, "Wage Distortion: Why America's Top Female College Graduates Aren't Teaching," *Education Next* Spring (2005), 56.

27 Jean Protsik, "History of Teacher Pay and Incentive Reforms," *Journal of School Leadership* 6, no. 3 (1996).
28 "History of Teacher Pay," Consortium for Policy Research in Education at the University of Wisconsin-Madison, http://www.wcer.wisc.edu/CPRE/tcomp/general/teacherpay.php (accessed June 15, 2008).
29 Ferguson and Ladd, "How and Why Money Matters," 278.
30 Rivkin, Hanushek and Kain, "Teachers, Schools, and Academic Achievement."
31 Ibid.
32 Charles T. Clotfelter, Helen F. Ladd and Jacob L. Vigdor, "Teacher-Student Matching and the Assessment of Teacher Effectiveness," *Journal of Human Resources* 41, no. 4 (2006).
33 Ibid., 793.
34 Charles T. Clotfelter, Helen F. Ladd and Jacob L. Vigdor. "Teacher Credentials and Student Achievement in High School: A Cross-Subject Analysis with Student Fixed Effects," National Center for Analysis of Longitudinal Data in Education Research, Working Paper 11, October (2007), http://www.caldercenter.org/PDF/1001104_Teacher_Credentials_HighSchool.pdf (accessed June 26, 2008).
35 Similar findings regarding the effectiveness of novice teachers can be found in Donald Boyd et al., "The Narrowing Gap in New York City Teacher Qualifications and Its Implications for Student Achievement in High-Poverty Schools" (Urban Institute, 2007), http://www.urban.org/url.cfm?ID=1001103 (accessed May 8, 2008).
36 Dan D. Goldhaber, "Everyone's Doing It, but What Does Teacher Testing Tell Us about Teacher Effectiveness?" (Urban Institute, 2007), 15, http://www.caldercenter.org/PDF/1001072_everyones_doing.PDF (accessed May 13, 2008).
37 Ibid.
38 Jay P. Greene, *Education Myths: What Special-Interest Groups Want You to Believe About Our Schools— and Why It Isn't So* (New York: Rowman & Littlefield Publishers, Inc., 2005).
39 Ibid. In making this claim, Greene refers to Kate Walsh, "Teacher Certification Reconsidered: Stumbling for Quality" (The Abell Foundation, 2002), http://www.abell.org/pubsitems/ed_cert_1101.pdf (accessed May 13, 2008).
40 Digest of Education Statistics 2007, "Table 64, Highest Degree Earned, Years of Full-Time Teaching Experience, and Average Class Size for Teachers in Public Elementary and Secondary Schools, by State: 2003-04" (National Center for Education Statistics, U.S. Department of Education, 2007), http://nces.ed.gov/programs/digest/d07/tables/dt07_064.asp?referrer=list (accessed May 13, 2008).
41 Protsik, "History of Teacher Pay and Incentive Reforms."
42 Goldhaber, "The Mystery of Good Teaching: Surveying the Evidence on Student Achievement and Teachers' Characteristics."
43 Ferguson and Ladd, "How and Why Money Matters," 278.
44 Hanushek and Rivkin, "How to Improve the Supply of High Quality Teachers"; Rivkin, Hanushek and Kain, "Teachers, Schools, and Academic Achievement."
45 Goldhaber, "Everyone's Doing It, but What Does Teacher Testing Tell Us about Teacher Effectiveness?," 14.

46   Goldhaber, "The Mystery of Good Teaching: Surveying the Evidence on Student Achievement and Teachers' Characteristics," 53.

47   Ibid, 54.

48   See MCL 380.1531 (general rule), MCL 380.505(2) (allowing limited exceptions for charter schools).

49   "The Secretary's Fifth Annual Report on Teacher Quality: A Highly Qualified Teacher in Every School Classroom" (Office of Postsecondary Preparation, U.S. Department of Education, 2006), http://www.ed.gov/about/reports/annual/teachprep/2006-title2report.pdf (accessed May 13, 2008).

50   Mich. Admin. Code r. 390.1101(a).

51   "Frequently Asked Questions for MTTC," Michigan Department of Education, http://www.michigan.gov/mde/0,1607,7-140-6530_5683_5857-116214--,00.html (accessed June 10, 2008).

52   Mich. Admin. Code, r. 390.115(3).

53   "Frequently Asked Questions" (Michigan Department of Education Office of Professional Preparation Services, 2005), http://www.michigan.gov/documents/faq_21180_7.pdf (accessed May 15, 2008).

54   Jess Castle and Sandi Jacobs, "State Teacher Policy Yearbook - Progress on Teacher Quality" (National Council on Teacher Quality, 2007), http://www.nctq .org/stpy/reports/stpy_national.pdf (accessed September 11, 2007). This report contains detailed information on Michigan teacher preparation and licensure requirements.

55   Michigan Teacher Certification Code, R. 390.1126.

56   Ibid. at 390.1127.

57   Ibid. at 390.1123(2). "The applicant shall present evidence of participation [in] a supervised directed teaching experience at the level for which the certificate is to be granted. The directed teaching assignment shall be for a minimum duration of 12 weeks and for a minimum of 6 semester credit hours."

58   Mike Flanagan, "Report on Teacher Preparation Institution Performance Scores" (Michigan Department of Education, 2007), http://www.michigan.gov/documents/mde/Item_W_204559_7.pdf (accessed May 15, 2008).

59   "Minutes: State Board of Education: August 7, 2007" (Michigan Department of Education, 2007), http://www.michigan.gov/documents/mde/MinutesAug07_208791_7.pdf (accessed June 14, 2008).

60   Ibid.

61   Linda Darling-Hammond et al., "Does Teacher Preparation Matter? Evidence About Teacher Certification, Teach for America, and Teacher Effectiveness," *Education Policy Analysis Archives* 13, no. 42 (2005).

62   Ibid.

63   In asserting that teacher education and certification positively impact student achievement, the authors cite Dan D. Goldhaber and D. J. Brewer, "Does Teacher Certification Matter? High School Teacher Certification Status and Student Achievement," *Educational Evaluation and Policy Analysis* 22 (2000): 129-45; P. Hawk, C. Coble and M. Swanson, "Certification: It Does Matter," *Journal of Teacher Education* 36, no. 3 (1985): 13-15; David H. Monk, "Subject Area

Preparation of Secondary Mathematics and Science Teachers and Student Achievement," *Economics of Education Review* 13, no. 2 (1994); R.P. Strauss and E.A. Sawyer, "Some New Evidence on Teacher and Student Competencies," *Economics of Education Review* 5, no. 1 (1986); Harold Wenglinsky, "How Teaching Matters: Bringing the Classroom Back into Discussions of Teacher Quality" (The Milken Family Foundation and Educational Testing Service, 2000), http://www.ets.org/Media/Education_Topics/pdf/teamat.pdf (accessed May 15, 2008); Suzanne Wilson, Robert Floden, and Joan Ferrini-Mundy, "Teacher Preparation Research: Current Knowledge, Gaps, and Recommendations" (Center for the Study of Teaching and Policy and Michigan State University, 2001), http://depts.washington.edu/ctpmail/PDFs/TeacherPrep-WFFM-02-2001.pdf (accessed May 15, 2008).

64   Goldhaber, "Everyone's Doing It, but What Does Teacher Testing Tell Us about Teacher Effectiveness?" 14.

65   Hanushek and Rivkin, "How to Improve the Supply of High Quality Teachers"; Robert Gordon, Thomas J. Kane and Douglas O. Staiger, "Identifying Effective Teachers Using Performance on the Job" (Brookings Institute, 2006), http://www.brookings.edu/views/papers/200604hamilton_1.pdf (accessed May 16, 2008); Christopher Jepsen and Steven G. Rivkin, "What Is the Tradeoff Between Smaller Classes and Teacher Quality" (National Bureau of Economic Research, 2002), http://ssrn.com/abstract=332249 (accessed July 9, 2008). These authors also cite Eric Hanushek et al., "The Market for Teacher Quality," *American Economic Association Meetings* (Philadelphia: 2005); Ballou and Podgursky, "Reforming Teacher Preparation and Licensing: What Is the Evidence?"; Margaret Raymond, Stephen Fletcher and Javier Luque, "Teach for America: An Evaluation of Teacher Differences and Student Outcomes in Houston, Texas" (Thomas B. Fordham Foundation, 2001), http://credo.stanford.edu/downloads/tfa.pdf (accessed May 16, 2008); Thomas J. Kane, Jonah E. Rockoff and Douglas O. Staiger, "What Does Certification Tell Us About Teacher Effectiveness? Evidence from New York City" (Harvard Graduate School of Education, 2006), 1-66, http://www.dartmouth.edu/~dstaiger/Papers/nyc%20fellows%20march%202006.pdf (accessed May 16, 2008).

66   Kane, Rockoff and Staiger, "What Does Certification Tell Us About Teacher Effectiveness? Evidence from New York City," 1-66.

67   Ibid.

68   "Frequently Asked Questions" (NYC Teaching Fellows, 2008), http://www.nyctf.org/f_a_q/program_faq.html#aftertwoyears (accessed May 16, 2008).

69   Kane, Rockoff and Staiger, "What Does Certification Tell Us About Teacher Effectiveness? Evidence from New York City."

70   Paul T. Decker, Daniel P. Mayer and Steven Glazerman, "The Effects of Teach for America on Students: Findings from a National Evaluation" (Mathematica Policy Research, 2004), http://www.mathematica-mpr.com/publications/pdfs/teach.pdf (accessed May 16, 2008).

71   Susan Moore Johnson, Jill Harrison Berg and Morgaen L. Donaldson, "Who Stays in Teaching and Why: A Review of the Literature on Teacher Retention"

(The Project on the Next Generation of Teachers, Havard Graduate School of Education, 2005), http://assets.aarp.org/www.aarp.org_/articles/NRTA/Harvard_report.pdf (accessed May 16, 2008) also give the Mathematica study extra consideration. Thomas D. Cook uses a similar line of argument in Thomas D. Cook, "Considering the Major Arguments Against Random Assignment: An Analysis of the Intellectual Culture Surrounding Evaluation in American Schools of Education," *Harvard Faculty Seminar on Experiments in Education* (Cambridge, Mass.: 1999).

72   "About the MTTC: Program Overview," Pearson Education, Inc., http://www.mttc.nesinc.com/MI12_overview.asp (accessed May 16, 2008).

73   "Frequently Asked Questions for MTTC," http://www.michigan.gov/mde/0,1607,7-140-6530_5683_5857-116214--,00.html#mttc2 (accessed May 16, 2007).

74   Ibid.

75   Ruth Mitchell and Patte Barth, "How Teacher Licensing Tests Fall Short," *Thinking K-16* Volume 3, Issue 1 (The Education Trust, 1999), http://www2 .edtrust.org/NR/rdonlyres/5F7B8FCA-2400-47DE-9C40-AC948D934836/0/k16_spring99.pdf (accessed June 27, 2008).

76   Sandra Stotsky, "Teacher Licensure Tests: Their Relationship to Mathematics Teachers' Academic Competence and Student Achievement in Mathematics" (Education Working Paper Archive, 2007), http://www.uark.edu/ua/der/EWPA/Research/Teacher_Quality/1798.html (accessed May 16, 2007).

77   "The Secretary's Fifth Annual Report on Teacher Quality: A Highly Qualified Teacher in Every School Classroom."

78   "Frequently Asked Questions for MTTC," Question Number Three: "Michigan law requires that teacher candidates for Michigan's initial, provisional teaching certification must pass all three subtests of the Basic Skills test before enrolling in student teaching. Some colleges and universities require a passing score on all three Basic Skills subtests for admission into a teacher preparation program," http://www.michigan.gov/mde/0,1607,7-140-6530_5683_5857-116214--,00. html#mttc2 (accessed May 16, 2007).

79   Michael P. Flanagan, "Report on Teacher Preparation Institution Scores" (Michigan Department of Education, 2007), http://www.michigan.gov/documents/mde/Item_W_204559_7.pdf (accessed May 22, 2008).

80   Sandra Stotsky, "Why American Students Do Not Learn to Read Very Well: The Unintended Consequences of Title II and Teacher Testing," *Independent Education Review: The Journal on Education Policy* 2, no. 2 (2006): 6.

81   Ibid.: 8.

82   Clotfelter, Ladd and Vigdor, "Teacher-Student Matching and the Assessment of Teacher Effectiveness."

83   Ibid, 799.

84   Goldhaber, "Everyone's Doing It, but What Does Teacher Testing Tell Us about Teacher Effectiveness?"; Hanushek and Rivkin, "How to Improve the Supply of High Quality Teachers."

85   Ibid.

86   Stotsky, "Teacher Licensure Tests: Their Relationship to Mathematics Teachers' Academic Competence and Student Achievement in Mathematics."
87   Dale Ballou and Michael Podgursky, "Recruiting Smarter Teachers," *Journal of Human Resources* 30, no. 2 (1995): 326-38.
88   Ibid.
89   Loeb and Reininger, "Public Policy and Teacher Labor Markets: What We Know and Why It Matters."
90   Reg Weaver, "Opposing View: Reject Federal Pay Mandates" (USA Today, 2007), http://blogs.usatoday.com/oped/2007/09/opposing-view-r.html (accessed May 16, 2008).
91   "NEA Student Program" (National Education Association), http://www.nea.org/student-program/about/state2.html#michigan (accessed May 16, 2008).
92   Nick Bunkley, "Michigan Government Shutdown Ends," *The New York Times*, October 1, 2007, http://www.nytimes.com/2007/10/01/us/01cnd-michigan.html?_r=2&oref=slogin&oref=slogin (accessed June 26, 2008).
93   Reg Weaver, "No Child Left Behind," *The New York Times*, September 10, 2007, http://www.nytimes.com/2007/09/10/opinion/lweb10teachers.html?_r=2&oref=slogin&oref=slogin (accessed June 26, 2008).
94   "The Class-Size Reduction Program: Boosting Achievement in Schools across the Nation. A First Year Report" (U.S. Department of Education, 2001), http://www.ed.gov/offices/OESE/ClassSize/class.pdf (accessed May 16, 2008).
95   Douglas Harris, "Class Size and School Size: Taking the Trade-Offs Seriously," *Brookings Papers on Education Policy 2006-2007*, ed. Frederick Hess and Tom Loveless (Washington, D.C.: Brookings Institution, 2007), 137-61.
96   Ibid., 153.
97   Rivkin, Hanushek and Kain, "Teachers, Schools, and Academic Achievement."
98   Ibid., 447.
99   "Class Size Reduction in California: The 1998-99 Evaluation Findings" (CSR Research Consortium), http://www.classize.org/summary/98-99/index.htm (accessed May 16, 2008).
100 Rivkin, Hanushek and Kain, "Teachers, Schools, and Academic Achievement," 447.
101 Ibid.
102 Greene, *Education Myths: What Special-Interest Groups Want You to Believe About Our Schools— and Why It Isn't So*, 55.
103 "Class Size Reduction in California: The 1998-99 Evaluation Findings."
104 Ibid.
105 Ibid.
106 Ibid.
107 Ibid.
108 "Statistical Tables: Public Elementary-Secondary Education Finances: 1998-99" (U.S. Census Bureau, 1999), http://ftp2.census.gov/govs/school/99tables.pdf (accessed May 17, 2008).
109 B.J. Biddle and David C. Berliner, "Class Size, School Size," *Educational Leadership* 59, no. 5 (2002).

110 Ibid.
111 Greene, *Education Myths: What Special-Interest Groups Want You to Believe About Our Schools— and Why It Isn't So*, 50.
112 Harris, "Class Size and School Size: Taking the Trade-Offs Seriously," 137.
113 Ibid., 140-42.
114 Ibid., 140-44.
115 Ibid., 147.
116 Ibid., 139.
117 "Rankings & Estimates, Rankings of the States 2005 and Estimates of School Statistics 2006" (National Education Association, 2006), http://www.nea.org/edstats/images/06rankings.pdf (accessed May 17, 2008).
118 "Michigan State Profile" (National Center for Education Statistics, 2006), http://nces.ed.gov/naep3/states/profile.asp (accessed May 17, 2008).
119 Terry M. Moe, "Political Control and the Power of the Agent," *Journal of Law, Economics, and Organization* 22, no. 1 (2006).
120 Harris, "Class Size and School Size: Taking the Trade-Offs Seriously," 154.
121 Greene, *Education Myths: What Special-Interest Groups Want You to Believe About Our Schools— and Why It Isn't So*, 51.
122 "Proven Methods, Highly Qualified Teachers for Every Child" (U.S. Department of Education, 2006), http://www.ed.gov/nclb/methods/teachers/stateplanfacts.html (accessed May 18, 2008).
123 This reform is also suggested by Gordon, Kane and Staiger, "Identifying Effective Teachers Using Performance on the Job"; Hanushek and Rivkin, "How to Improve the Supply of High Quality Teachers"; Murnane and Steele, "What Is the Problem? The Challenge of Providing Effective Teachers for All Children"; "Teaching at Risk: Progress and Potholes" (The Teaching Commission); Castle and Jacobs, "State Teacher Policy Yearbook - Progress on Teacher Quality."
124 Castle and Jacobs, "State Teacher Policy Yearbook - Progress on Teacher Quality."
125 McCaffrey et al., "Models for Value-Added Modeling of Teacher Effects," 68.
126 Murnane and Steele, "What Is the Problem? The Challenge of Providing Effective Teachers for All Children." The National Center for Teaching Quality highlights similar limitations.
127 Dale Ballou, "Sizing up Test Scores," *Education Next* 2, no. 2 (2002).
128 "MEAP Assessment Administrator Manual, Grades 3-9, Fall 2007" (Michigan Department of Education, Michigan Educational Assessment Program, 2007), http://www.michigan.gov/documents/mde/MEAP_Admin_Manual_F07_FINAL_205351_7.pdf (accessed July 9, 2008).
129 Gordon, Kane and Staiger, "Identifying Effective Teachers Using Performance on the Job," 21.
130 Ibid.
131 Ibid.
132 "NWEA Members: Michigan" (Northwest Evaluation Association, 2008), http://www.nwea.org/about/members.asp?stateCode=MI (accessed May 13, 2008).
133 John Cronin, spokesman for the Northwest Evaluation Association, E-mail correspondence with Marc Holley, April 2, 2008.

134 Richard Buddin et al., "Merit Pay for Florida Teachers: Design and Implementation Issues" (RAND Working Papers, 2007), http://rand.org/pubs/working_papers/2007/RAND_WR508.pdf (accessed May 18, 2008).
135 Ibid. In this summary, Buddin et al. point to the findings of Brian Jacob and Lars Lefgren, "Principals as Agents: Subjective Performance Measurement in Education," in *Faculty Research Working Papers Series* (Harvard University, John F. Kennedy School of Government, 2005).
136 Jacob and Lefgren, "Principals as Agents: Subjective Performance Measurement in Education," 8.
137 Ibid., 3.
138 Ibid., 9.
139 Ibid., 22-23.
140 Ibid.
141 Douglas Harris and Tim Sass, "What Makes for a Good Teacher and Who Can Tell," *APPAM Conference* (Washington, D.C.: 2007), 1-35.
142 Ibid., 1.
143 Michael Podgursky and Matthew G. Springer, "Teacher Performance Pay: A Review" (National Center on Performance Incentives, 2006), http://www.performanceincentives.org/data/files/news/PapersNews/Podgursky_and_Springer_2006_Revised.pdf (accessed May 18, 2008).
144 "Districts Report Some Success on Teacher Pay Incentives," *Michigan Education Report*, May 24, 2007, http://www.educationreport.org/8497 (accessed June 26, 2008).
145 Allan Odden et al., "Enhancing Teacher Quality through Knowledge- and Skills-Based Pay" (Consortium for Policy Research in Education, 2001), http://www.wcer.wisc.edu/CPRE/publications/rb34.pdf (accessed May 18, 2008).
146 Herbert Heneman, Anthony Milanowski and Steven Kimball, "Teacher Performance Pay: Synthesis of Plans, Research, and Guidelines for Practice" (Consortium for Policy Research in Education, 2007), http://www.eric.ed.gov/ERICDocs/data/ericdocs2sql/content_storage_01/0000019b/80/33/59/0d.pdf (accessed May 18, 2008).
147 Ibid.
148 Ibid.
149 David J. Hoff, "Unions, Miller Spar over Teacher Pay," *Education Week*, September 10, 2007, http://blogs.edweek.org/edweek/NCLB-ActII/2007/09/testy_merit_pay_exchange.html (accessed June 26, 2008).
150 Ibid.
151 David N. Figlio and Lawrence Kenny "Individual Teacher Incentives and Student Performance," *NBER Working Paper No. 12627*, 10 (National Bureau of Economic Research, 2006), http://www.nber.org/papers/w12627.pdf?new_window=1.
152 Ibid., 13.
153 Ibid., 14.
154 Lewis C. Solmon and Michael Podgursky, "The Pros and Cons of Performance-Based Compensation" (Milken Family Foundation, 2000), http://www.mff.org/pubs/Pros_cons.pdf (accessed may 18, 2008); Joshua H. Barnett, "How Does Merit

Pay Change Schools" (Dissertation, University of Arkansas, 2007); Podgursky and Springer, "Teacher Performance Pay: A Review"; Marc Holley, Joshua H. Barnett and Gary W. Ritter, "Merit Pay: A Discussion of the Issues" (Office for Education Policy, University of Arkansas, 2007), http://www.uark.edu/ua/oep/policy_briefs/2007/Policy_Brief_10_Merit_Pay.pdf (accessed May 18, 2008); Heneman, Milanowski and Kimball, "Teacher Performance Pay: Synthesis of Plans, Research, and Guidelines for Practice."

155 Marcus A. Winters et al., "An Evaluation of Teacher Performance Pay in Arkansas" (Department of Education Reform, University of Arkansas, 2007), http://www.uark.edu/ua/der/Research/performance_pay_ar.html (accessed May 18, 2008); Gary W. Ritter et al., "Year Two Evaluation of the Achievement Challenge Pilot Project in the Little Rock Public School District" (Department of Education Reform, University of Arkansas, 2008), http://uark.edu/ua/der/Research/merit_pay/year_two/Full_Report_with_Appendices.pdf (accessed May 18, 2008).

156 Winters et al., "An Evaluation of Teacher Performance Pay in Arkansas."

157 Ritter et al., "Year Two Evaluation of the Achievement Challenge Pilot Project in the Little Rock Public School District," 3-4.

158 Ibid., 6.

159 Ibid.

160 Ibid.

161 Ibid.

162 Charles T. Clotfelter and Helen F. Ladd, "Recognizing and Rewarding Success in Public Schools," *Holding Schools Accountable: Performance-Based Reform in Education*, ed. Helen F. Ladd, 27 (Brookings Institution, 1996).

163 Carolyn B. Horan and Vicki Lambert, "Evaluation of Utah Career Ladder Programs" (Beryl Buck Institute for Education, 1994), http://eric.ed.gov/ERICDocs/data/ericdocs2sql/content_storage_01/0000019b/80/15/8a/93.pdf (accessed May 19, 2008).

164 Carolyn Hoxby and Andrew Leigh, "Wage Distortion: Why America's Top Female College Graduates Aren't Teaching."

165 Clotfelter and Ladd, "Recognizing and Rewarding Success in Public Schools," *Holding Schools Accountable: Performance-Based Reform in Education*.

166 "Teacher Incentive Fund" (U.S. Department of Education, 2007), http://www.ed.gov/programs/teacherincentive/awards.html (accessed May 18, 2008).

167 David H. Monk, "Recruiting and Retaining High-Quality Teachers in Rural Areas," *The Future of Children* 17, no. 1 (2007).

168 "Professional Compensation" (American Federation of Teachers), http://www.aft.org/topics/teacher-quality/comp.htm (accessed May 19, 2008).

169 Hanushek and Rivkin, "How to Improve the Supply of High Quality Teachers"; Stotsky and Haverty, "Can a State Department of Education Increase Teacher Quality? Lessons Learned in Massachusetts."

170 Frederick Hess, "Teacher Quality, Teacher Pay" (Hoover Institution, 2004), http://www.hoover.org/publications/policyreview/3438676.html (accessed May 19, 2008).

171 Dan D. Goldhaber, Kate Destler and Dan Player, "Teacher Labor Markets and the
     Perils of Using Hedonics to Estimate Compensating Differentials in the Public
     Sector" (Center on Reinventing Public Education, 2007), http://www.crpe.org/cs/
     crpe/download/csr_files/wp_sfrp17_goldhaber_aug07.pdf
     (accessed May 19, 2008).
172 Kenneth M. Braun, "An Analysis of Proposal 5: The 'K-16' Michigan Ballot
     Measure" (Mackinac Center for Public Policy, 2006), http://www.mackinac.org/
     archives/2006/s2006-05.pdf (accessed June 26, 2008).
173 Ryan S. Olson and Michael D. LaFaive, "A Michigan School Money Primer"
     (Mackinac Center for Public Policy, 2007) 99, 109, http://www.mackinac.org/
     archives/2007/s2007-04.pdf (accessed June 26, 2008).
174 "NCLB Revised Highly Qualified Teacher State Plan." The NCTQ credits
     Michigan for having this plan.
175 Benjamin J. Keys and Thomas S. Dee, "Dollars and Sense: What a Tennessee
     Experiment Tells Us About Merit Pay," *Education Next* 5, no. 1 (2005).
176 Ibid., 63.
177 Ibid., 66-67.
178 Horan and Lambert, "Evaluation of Utah Career Ladder Programs," 1-160.
179 Ibid., 24
180 Johnson, Berg and Donaldson, "Who Stays in Teaching and Why: A Review of the
     Literature on Teacher Retention."
181 "The Four Elements of TAP" (National Institute for Excellence in Teaching, 2008),
     http://www.talentedteachers.org/tap.taf?page=fourelements
     (accessed May 19, 2008).
182 Matthew Springer, Dale Ballou and Art Peng, "Impact of the Teacher
     Advancement Program on Student Test Score Gains: Findings from an
     Independent Appraisal" (National Center on Performance Incentives, 2008),
     Abstract, http://www.performanceincentives.org/data/files/news/PapersNews/
     Springer_et_al_2008.pdf (accessed July 9, 2008).
183 Ibid.
184 "The Secretary's Fifth Annual Report on Teacher Quality: A Highly Qualified
     Teacher in Every School Classroom."
185 Ibid.
186 Ibid.
187 Ibid.
188 Castle and Jacobs, "State Teacher Policy Yearbook - Progress on Teacher Quality."
189 Ibid., 78.
190 "Frequently Asked Questions" (NYC Teaching Fellows, 2008), http://www.nyctf
     .org/f_a_q/program_faq.html#aftertwoyears (accessed May 16, 2008).
191 "Program History and Statistics," (NYC Teaching Fellows, 2007),
     http://www.nyctf.org/about/history.html (accessed May 21, 2008).
192 Ibid.
193 See George C. Leef's editorial from 2002 on Teach for America: "'Teach for
     America' Success Points the Way to Teacher Certification Reform" (Mackinac
     Center for Public Policy, 2002), http://www.mackinac.org/4045 (accessed

May 21, 2008); "Top Grads from Class of 2002 Turn to Service," (Teach For America, 2002), http://www.teachforamerica.org/newsroom/documents/ TeachForAmerica_News_20020507.html (accessed May 21, 2008).

194 Bess Keller, "Teach for America Operation to Close in Detroit," *Education Week*, April 21, 2004, http://www.edweek.org/ew/articles/2004/04/21/32tfa.h23.html?qs =Teach+for+America+Operation+to+Close+in+Detroit (accessed July 9, 2008).

195 "Regions" (Teach For America, 2008), http://www.teachforamerica.org/about/ regions/index.htm (accessed May 21, 2008).

196 Stotsky, "Teacher Licensure Tests: Their Relationship to Mathematics Teachers' Academic Competence and Student Achievement in Mathematics."

197 Ibid.

198 Castle and Jacobs, "State Teacher Policy Yearbook - Progress on Teacher Quality."

199 Ibid., 40.

200 "American Board for Certification of Teacher Excellence" (American Board for Certification of Teacher Excellence, 2008), http://www.abcte.org/ (accessed May 21, 2008).

201 Ibid.

202 Ibid.

203 Steven Glazerman and Christina Tuttle, "An Evaluation of American Board Teacher Certification: Progress and Plans" (Mathematica Policy Research, Inc., 2006), http://www.eric.ed.gov/ERICDocs/data/ericdocs2sql/content_ storage_01/0000019b/80/28/09/9c.pdf (accessed May 21, 2008).

204 Steven Glazerman, Christina Tuttle and Gail Baxter, "School Principals' Perspectives on the Passport to Teaching" (Mathematica Policy Research, Inc., 2006), http://www.abcte.org/files/2006_principal_survey.pdf (accessed May 21, 2008).

205 John E. Chubb and Terry M. Moe, *Politics, Markets, and America's Schools* (Brookings Institution, 1990), 187.

206 Jessica Levin, Jennifer Mulhern and Joan Schunck, "Unintended Consequences: The Case for Reforming the Staffing Rules in Urban Teachers' Union Contracts" (The New Teacher Project, 2005), http://www.tntp.org/newreport/TNTP%20 Unintended%20Consequences.pdf (accessed June 26, 2008).

207 Frederick Hess and Coby Loup, "The Leadership Limbo: Teacher Labor Agreements in America's Fifty Largest School Districts" (The Thomas Fordham Institute, 2008), http://www.edexcellence.net/doc/leadershiplimbo/the_ leadership_limbo.pdf (accessed June 26, 2008).

208 Steven Adamowski, Susan Bowles Therriault and Anthony Cavanna, "The Autonomy Gap: Barriers to Effective School Leadership" (Thomas B. Fordham Institute, 2007), 17, http://eric.ed.gov/ERICDocs/data/ericdocs2sql/content_ storage_01/0000019b/80/2b/6f/62.pdf (accessed June 25, 2008).

209 Ibid., 18.

210 Loeb and Reininger, "Public Policy and Teacher Labor Markets: What We Know and Why It Matters"; Murnane and Steele, "What Is the Problem? The Challenge of Providing Effective Teachers for All Children"; Hamilton Lankford, Susanna Loeb and James Wyckoff, "Teacher Sorting and the Plight of Urban Schools: A Descriptive Analysis," *Educational Evaluation and Policy Analysis* 24,

no. 1 (2002); Donald Boyd et al., "Explaining the Short Careers of High-Achieving Teachers in Schools with Low-Performing Students," *American Economic Review* 95, no. 2 (2005).

211 Marguerite Roza and Paul T. Hill, "How Within-District Spending Inequities Help Some Schools to Fail" (Brookings Institution, 2004); Hanushek and Rivkin, "How to Improve the Supply of High Quality Teachers" also make this point.

212 Roza and Hill, "How Within-District Spending Inequities Help Some Schools to Fail."

213 Ibid.

214 MCL 38.81(1); MCL 38.91(1).

215 MCL 38.71; MSA 15.1971, § 1(4). The Teachers' Tenure Act generally does not cover teachers in public school academies.

216 MCL 38.81(1); MCL 38.91(1).

217 For similar recommendations, see "Teaching at Risk: Progress and Potholes" (The Teaching Commission), http://www.nctq.org/nctq/images/ttc_teachingatrisk.pdf (accessed July 9, 2008).

218 Weaver, "Opposing View: Reject Federal Pay Mandates." Weaver has argued, "We should invest precious federal dollars in giving all teachers competitive salaries, quality professional development and better working conditions." See also Linda Darling-Hammond, "A Marshall Plan for Teaching," *Education Week*, January 10, 2007, http://www.edweek.org/ew/articles/2007/01/10/18hammond.h26.html?print=1 (accessed July 9, 2008).

219 According to the MDE, "During the 3 year period, the teacher shall also receive intensive professional development induction into teaching, based on a professional development plan that is consistent with the requirements of Section 3a of Article II of Act 4 of the Public Acts of the Extra Session of 1937 being Section 38.83a of Michigan Compiled Laws including classroom management and instructional delivery." See "A Few Clarifying Thoughts on Section 1526" (Michigan Department of Education, 1997), http://www.michigan.gov/mde/0,1607,7-140-5235_6947-32578--,00.html (accessed May 21, 2008).

220 Michael S. Garet et al., "What Makes Professional Development Effective? Results from a National Sample of Teachers," *American Education Research Journal* 38, no. 4 (2001); Heather C. Hill, "Learning in the Teaching Workforce," *The Future of Children* 17, no. 1 (2007).

221 Loeb and Reininger, "Public Policy and Teacher Labor Markets: What We Know and Why It Matters."

222 Hill, "Learning in the Teaching Workforce."

223 MCL 380.1250.

INDEX

MACKINAC CENTER
F O R   P U B L I C   P O L I C Y

BOARD OF DIRECTORS

D. Joseph Olson, Chairman
*Senior Vice President and General
Counsel, Amerisure Companies*

Lawrence W. Reed, President
Mackinac Center for Public Policy

Joseph J. Fitzsimmons
*Retired President,
University Microfilms*

Hon. Paul V. Gadola
U.S. District Court Judge

Kent B. Herrick
President and CEO, Thermogy

Richard G. Haworth
*Chairman of the Board,
Haworth, Inc.*

Phil F. Jenkins
Chairman, Sweepster Inc.

Edward C. Levy Jr.
President, Edw. C. Levy Co.

Rodney M. Lockwood Jr.
*President, Lockwood
Construction Company, Inc.*

Joseph P. Maguire
*President,
Wolverine Development
Corporation*

Richard D. McLellan
Attorney, Dykema Gossett

John E. Riecker
*of Counsel to Braun, Kendrick,
Finkbeiner, PLC*

James M. Rodney
*Chairman of the Board,
Detroit Forming Inc.*

Linda K. Rodney
*Attorney at Law, Law Offices
of Linda K. Rodney, P.C.*

BOARD OF SCHOLARS

Dr. Donald Alexander
Western Michigan University

Dr. William Allen
Michigan State University

Dr. Thomas Bertonneau
Writer and Independent Scholar

Dr. Brad Birzer
Hillsdale College

Dr. Peter Boettke
George Mason University

Dr. Theodore Bolema
Central Michigan University

Dr. Stephen Colarelli
Central Michigan University

Andrew Coulson
Cato Institute

Robert Crowner
Eastern Michigan University (ret.)

Dr. Richard Cutler
University of Michigan (ret.)

Dr. Richard Ebeling
*Foundation for Economic
Education*

Dr. Jefferson Edgens
Morehead State University

Dr. David Felbeck
University of Michigan (ret.)

Dr. Burton Folsom
Hillsdale College

Dr. Wayland Gardner
Western Michigan University (ret.)

John Grether
Northwood University

Dr. Michael Heberling
Baker College

Dr. Ormand Hook
*Mecosta-Osceola Intermediate
School District*

Robert Hunter
Mackinac Center for Public Policy

Prof. Harry Hutchison
Wayne State University

Dr. David Janda
*Institute for Preventative
Sports Medicine*

Annette Kirk
*Russell Kirk Center for
Cultural Renewal*

David Littmann
Mackinac Center for Public Policy

Dr. Dale Matcheck
Northwood University

Dr. Paul McCracken
University of Michigan (ret.)

Charles Meiser
*Lake Superior
State University (ret.)*

Glenn Moots
Northwood University

Dr. George Nastas III
Marketing Consultants

Dr. John Pafford
Northwood University

Dr. Mark Perry
University of Michigan - Flint

Gregory Rehmke
*Economic Thinking/
E Pluribus Unum Films*

Dr. Steve Safranek
Ave Maria School of Law

Dr. Howard Schwartz
Oakland University

James Sheehan
Deutsche Bank Securities

Rev. Robert Sirico
*Acton Institute for the
Study of Religion and Liberty*

Dr. Bradley Smith
Capital University Law School

Dr. John Taylor
Grand Valley State University

Dr. Richard K. Vedder
Ohio University

Prof. Harry Veryser Jr.
University of Detroit Mercy

John Walter Jr.
Dow Corning Corporation (ret.)

Dr. William Wilson
Economic Consultant

Mike Winther
Institute for Principle Studies

Dr. Gary Wolfram
Hillsdale College